How to Make Money with AI for Beginners

The Step-by-Step Guide to Creating Multiple Passive Income Streams

Updated for OpenAI ChatGPT-5 and Claude 4

Now includes **The PROMPT Goldmine System™**

By

Brian Scott Fitzgerald

Published By Fitzgerald Publishing Group

How to Make Money Online: THE SERIES

I created a series of 12 (twelve) books on How to Make Money Online.

Feel free to read any of my books in the series, which can be found on my Author page on Amazon

You can visit this link or Scan this QR code to get access

https://www.amazon.com/author/brianscottfitzgerald.

Contents

Your Free Gift.

Thank you for your purchase; I'm offering my readers the FREE PDF version of ChatGPT Prompts.

To get almost instant access, go to this website.
https://go.fitzgeraldpublishing.com/opt-in-page-make-money-ai

Or use your phone to take a picture of this QR code, and it will take you to the Website for your Gift.

Inside the book, you will discover:

- **3000 Prompts** To help you make even more money online.
- **Save time:** You can search for new topics to create content on ChatGPT.
- **Expand knowledge:** Our Package of ChatGPT Prompts covers various topics, from science and technology to art and culture.

If you want to make even more money online, grab this free PDF.

Wait, that's not all; just for buying this book and getting the free PDF above, you can also earn another free Book.

You can use your phone to take a picture of this QR code.

Use the latest AI techniques to uncover online innovation's future. Take advantage! "Beyond ChatGPT and 50 New AI Tools: The Ultimate Guide to Discovering Cutting-Edge AI Tools Beyond ChatGPT" offers endless possibilities. Explore a variety of cutting-edge AI solutions to transform your work. Discover advanced AI tools beyond ChatGPT on this thrilling voyage.

Grab this free book if you want to make even more money online.

Introduction

This is my second book on Artificial Intelligence, and the pace of change still catches me off guard. In the short time since my first book on ChatGPT and AI was published, the landscape has shifted again. New tools have appeared, older ones have evolved, and opportunities to make money with AI have multiplied. I've spent these months learning, testing, and refining my understanding so I can pass on what's real, what works, and what's worth your time.

If you've never used ChatGPT or any other AI tool, you're not behind. You don't need technical expertise to understand what's ahead. My goal here isn't to bury you in academic language or buzzwords; it's to make sure you can see how AI fits into your work, your ideas, and your ability to earn online.

We're going to explore what's possible now, and what's on the horizon. This isn't just about the flashiest tools or the latest trends — it's about practical uses you can start applying today. Think of it as sitting down with someone who's spent the late nights clicking through menus, testing prompts, and breaking a few things to see what happens — so you don't have to.

A Practical Starting Point

AI is no longer a novelty in tech circles. It's embedded in email clients, search engines, design platforms, and even small business software. Used right, it can automate repetitive work, give you new creative angles, and save hours every week. Used poorly, it can create errors, waste time, and drain money. This book is about that middle ground — where human judgment and machine speed make sense together.

Maybe you're here because your business needs better content. Perhaps you're trying to speed up research or find more innovative ways to generate sales. Maybe you're curious about creating something new entirely — a product, a service, or a brand — without the overhead you'd face a decade ago. Those are all within reach, and we'll break down how.

Beyond ChatGPT

If you've read my earlier book *Making Money Online with ChatGPT*, you'll know I focused heavily on one tool. That still matters — ChatGPT remains a strong all-purpose assistant — but it's not the whole picture anymore. In just a few months, we've seen specialized AI services for image creation, video editing, data analysis, voice generation, code building, and more. Some are designed for broad use, while others are tailored for specific industries. In this book, we'll cover how to use multiple tools together to create something bigger than the sum of its parts.

And no — this isn't a technical manual. You won't have to read Python scripts or memorize complex workflows. I'll explain features in plain terms, then show you examples of how they can work for both solo creators and established businesses.

Why AI is Worth Your Attention

AI has a speed advantage you can't ignore. It can sort through thousands of data points faster than you can skim through one spreadsheet. It can summarize, rewrite, and restructure information without losing focus or complaining. That doesn't make it infallible — you'll see me point out plenty of mistakes AI can make — but it changes what's possible in terms of scale.

A small business can run targeted ad campaigns without hiring a whole marketing team. A freelance designer can generate concept art in minutes instead of days. A writer can produce structured drafts before coffee gets cold. These aren't theoretical. They're things people are doing right now, and in many cases, for less than the cost of a single lunch out.

For Creators and Businesses Alike

You might think AI is mainly for tech-driven companies, but creators are finding just as much value. A musician can feed reference tracks into a composition model to test new styles. A podcaster can auto-generate transcripts and social clips. A teacher can build customized lesson plans in minutes. The point isn't replacing skill — it's about removing the time-consuming parts that stop you from focusing on the real work.

I've seen people use AI to overcome creative blocks, brainstorm dozens of product names, or test headlines before launching a campaign. The real magic isn't the output itself — it's the momentum that output creates.

Cutting Through the Hype

You've probably noticed the flood of "AI will change everything" headlines. Some of that's true. A lot isn't. You'll also find people selling tools they barely understand or promising you passive income streams without showing the hard work behind them. This book isn't about quick wins that disappear when the algorithm changes. It's about systems you can adapt as the tools change — because they will.

When I say, "AI can help you write a sales page," I'll show you the structure, the prompt, the output, and where it needs editing. When I say, "AI can help you research a market," I'll point to actual steps, not vague instructions.

A Reality Check

It's easy to get carried away with big promises. So, here's a truth: AI won't think for you. It won't care about your business goals, your creative standards, or your audience. It will generate possibilities. You'll need to judge which ones are worth using.

That's why we'll spend time on evaluation, not just how to produce output, but how to decide whether it's any good. Whether you're generating copy, designing visuals, or building a dataset, the ability to assess quality is what makes AI worth having in your toolkit.

What You'll Get from This Book

- A clear explanation of how AI fits into modern work.
- Examples that show the process from input to result.
- Guidance on combining tools without getting lost in complexity.
- Warnings about common pitfalls and how to avoid them.
- A realistic view of how AI can help you make money online.

Why I Wrote It This Way

AI didn't generate this book. Every section was researched, tested, and written by a human — me — because I believe the best use of these tools is still guided by human insight. AI can produce clean sentences and organized lists, but it won't catch nuance the way lived experience does. It doesn't know why a particular marketing hook will resonate or why a design feels balanced. Those are human calls.

And yes, I'll use AI examples in this book. I'll show you how I structure prompts, how I edit AI's work, and when I throw it out entirely. You'll see where it saves time, where it stumbles, and how I decide whether the trade-off is worth it.

The Bigger Picture

AI is still early in its public adoption. That means two things: the technology will continue to improve, and the people who learn how to use it now will be in a better position later. Whether you're building a side hustle, running a company, or just curious, you'll be ahead of most people simply by understanding what's possible.

We'll talk about fundamental tools you can use today — from AI writing assistants to image generators, data analyzers, and automation services — and we'll place them in context. Hence, you're not just chasing shiny objects. The goal isn't to use AI for everything; it's to use it where it gives you an edge.

So, as you read, think about the tasks you wish you could hand off. Consider the creative projects that sit half-finished because you ran out of time or energy. Think about the business processes that slow you down. Those are your openings.

By the time we're done, you'll not only know which tools can help, but how to put them to work without drowning in options. You'll see how to test ideas quickly, filter out the noise, and keep building momentum.

That's the promise of AI when you approach it with clear goals, a willingness to experiment, and the patience to refine. Not hype. Not magic. Just a more innovative way to work.

Before we get into the nuts and bolts of AI tools and workflows, I want to give you a map. A system. Something simple you can keep in your head while you read this book and while you put it into practice.

That system is called **The PROMPT Goldmine System™.**

Every time you see me talk about picking niches, researching, optimizing, or monetizing, this system is the invisible thread running through it. PROMPT isn't just a catchy word—it's a framework for turning AI into money.

Here's how it breaks down:

P – Position Your Niche. Most people go too broad. "I want to make money online" is vague. "I create AI-driven planners for new moms" is sharp. This step involves carving out the perfect slice of the internet pie, where demand is strong and competition is weak.

R – Research Winning Content. Why guess when you can reverse-engineer? With AI as your assistant, you can study what's already going viral, what's already selling, and what audiences already love. That's the research piece—find the winners and adapt the lessons.

O – Optimize with AI. AI doesn't print gold straight out of the box. You must refine it. With good prompts and clever editing, you can transform generic outputs into high-converting products, posts, and pitches. This is where prompt engineering meets polish.

M – Monetize via Platforms. Ideas are nice, but income comes from platforms. Etsy, Amazon KDP, Gumroad, YouTube, affiliate blogs—you'll see throughout this book how each platform can turn your AI outputs into actual cash flow.

P – Publish & Promote. Publishing alone isn't enough. You've got to ship your work out into the world and give it a push. AI can help with launching, scheduling, repurposing, and promoting content so that it reaches the right people instead of sitting on your hard drive.

T – Track & Tweak for Profit. If you're not measuring, you're guessing. Tracking lets you see what's working, what's flopping, and where the money is really coming from. Tweaking is how you compound profits over time. Together, this step makes sure your system doesn't just work once—it scales.

Think of this as the **backbone of the book.** Each chapter will show you specific tools, strategies, and case studies, but they'll all connect back to one of these six steps. By the time you finish, you'll not only understand AI—you'll have a repeatable system for building income streams.

So as you move forward, keep the word **PROMPT** in mind. It's your roadmap. It's your compass. And by the end of this book, it'll be second nature.

PART I

Foundations: Building Your AI Mindset and Skills

Before you start making money with AI, you need the basics down cold. Part I is where you build the foundation—understanding what AI can and cannot do, how the models work, and how to think about them in real business terms. These first four chapters are less about shiny tricks and more about giving you a compass.

- **Chapter 1** will strip away the hype. You'll see AI's real strengths and weaknesses, so you don't fall into the trap of expecting miracles or ignoring blind spots.
- **Chapter 2** digs into models and their limits—capabilities, constraints, and cost—because understanding these trade-offs is what keeps you profitable, not just fascinated.
- We'll pause for a **bonus update** on the state of AI today: GPT-5, Claude 3.5, Gemini, Mistral, and more. These tools evolve fast, and you'll see why some are worth using for heavy lifting while others shine in lighter workflows.

- **Chapter 3** is where you start learning how to talk to AI appropriately, prompting that actually survives model updates.
- **Chapter 4** closes Part I with your first AI workflow, built in under 30 minutes.

And here's where the **P – Position Your Niche** and the **O in PROMPT—Optimize with AI—comes in.**

Anyone can ask ChatGPT a question. Anyone can type a half-baked idea into an AI tool and get something back. But raw outputs are never the product. They're the starting point. Optimization is where you transform a rough response into something usable—something persuasive, polished, and profitable.

In these first chapters, you'll see why optimization is the real multiplier. It's not about using AI once and hoping for gold. It's about learning how to shape the outputs, refine them, and push them closer to what you need. That means better prompts, more effective editing, and more innovative use of tools.

Think of it this way: if you learn nothing else in Part I except how to optimize with AI, you'll already be ahead of 90% of casual users. Most people stop at the raw answer. You're going to learn how to keep going—turning drafts into deliverables, and ideas into assets. That's the O in PROMPT, and it's the thread running through this whole section.

CHAPTER 1

What AI Can and Cannot Do

Unlock the Secrets of AI

You can't use AI well without knowing where it's strong and where it falls short. This is where most people trip up. They either treat it like magic and expect perfection or dismiss it as useless because it made one bad mistake. Both views miss the point.

AI is a tool. A powerful one, yes, but still a tool. It's fast, it's flexible, and it can process more information in seconds than you could read in a week. But it doesn't "think" the way you do, and it's not meant to replace the messy, nuanced decision-making that humans bring to the table.

So, let's break it down — what it really can do, what it can't, and where you fit into the equation.

Core Concepts Without the Hype

Artificial Intelligence in this context mostly means systems that can generate, summarize, classify, or analyze information based on patterns they've learned from data. You've probably heard of ChatGPT, Claude, Gemini, or Midjourney. These are all specialized tools built on machine learning models.

Here's the thing: they're not "alive" or "thinking" in the human sense. They predict. Every word, image, or result they give you is based on probabilities — what's likely to come next given the input you've provided. That's why the same prompt can sometimes get slightly different answers.

AI works best when:

- The problem can be clearly described in text, numbers, or structured data.
- There's a large amount of relevant data to work with.
- The desired output can be judged against objective criteria.

This is why AI excels at tasks such as summarizing legal contracts, generating blog outlines, or classifying customer support requests. The rules of the task are implicit in the data, and the AI has enough examples to "guess" correctly most of the time.

Where AI Shines

Let's be real — AI does some things incredibly well, often at a scale or speed that's just not humanly possible.

1. Summarizing and Synthesizing Information

Give it a lengthy document, a transcript, or a dataset, and it can quickly extract the main points. For research-heavy work, this is a huge time-saver.

Example: A lawyer feeding in a 50-page deposition to get a bullet-point summary before diving into the full text.

2. Generating First Drafts

Whether it's marketing copy, a lesson plan, or product descriptions, AI can get you past the blank page problem. It's rarely perfect on the first try, but it's a starting point you can edit.

3. Brainstorming and Idea Expansion

You can throw half-baked ideas at it, and it'll give you variations, taglines, or possible directions. It's like having an assistant who never runs out of suggestions.

4. Pattern Recognition in Data

With the right tools, AI can spot trends you might miss — sales spikes tied to specific events, recurring customer complaints, or usage patterns in your product.

5. Language Translation and Style Adjustment

Modern AI models are surprisingly good at converting tone, simplifying jargon, or translating between languages — though still not perfect, especially for highly technical or culturally nuanced text.

Where AI Fails

Here's the part the hype often skips. AI has blind spots, and if you don't know them, you'll make bad decisions.

1. Accuracy Isn't Guaranteed

AI can "hallucinate" — that is, confidently state something completely wrong. This can occur in factual questions, citations, or numerical data. You can't unquestioningly accept output without verification.

2. Context Limits

Most AI models have a limit to how much information they can consider at once (the context window). Feed it too much, and earlier details get "forgotten."

3. Nuanced Judgment

It can't truly understand tone, intent, or subtext the way a human can. For example, it might miss sarcasm in customer feedback or the emotional weight of certain words.

4. Real-Time Awareness

Unless it's connected to live data, AI doesn't know what happened yesterday. Even when connected, it depends entirely on the sources it's given.

5. Ethics and Bias

AI reflects the data it's trained on — including the flaws and biases in that data. Without human oversight, it can reinforce stereotypes or make unfair assumptions.

The Human Role AI Can't Replace

No matter how fast or sophisticated AI gets, there are elements of judgment, creativity, and empathy that are still uniquely human. That's not a sentimental statement — it's a practical one.

You bring:

- **Critical Thinking** – Deciding if an answer makes sense.
- **Creativity with Constraints** – Knowing when to break patterns for originality.

- **Ethical Oversight** – Catching when output is biased or harmful.
- **Domain Knowledge** – Understanding your field in ways the AI can't replicate from text patterns alone.

Think of AI like a calculator for ideas. A calculator doesn't replace your ability to understand math — it just speeds up the work once you know what you're trying to solve.

Avoiding Common Missteps

Even experienced users make mistakes that limit AI's usefulness.

1. **Vague Inputs** – The AI's output is only as good as the detail in your request. "Write me a blog post" is less specific than "Write a 600-word post for small business owners on using AI to manage invoices, with three subheadings."
2. **Overreliance** – If you're letting AI handle entire processes without review, you're risking quality and trust.
3. **Ignoring Evaluation** – Good outputs get refined. Treat AI like an intern: review, edit, and give feedback (by refining prompts).
4. **Not Tracking Costs** – With API-based AI tools, costs can spike quickly if you're running large tasks repeatedly.

A Balanced Approach

Here's how to think about it:

- Automate repetitive, low-risk tasks (summaries, draft generation, formatting).

- Assist on higher-value work where AI can help with speed or structure, but you still control quality.
- Avoid handing off sensitive, high-risk decisions without a human in the loop.

In practice, this might look like:

- Using AI to produce the first draft of a client proposal → then adding custom examples and adjusting tone.
- Running AI to extract top complaints from 1,000 customer reviews → then deciding yourself what product changes to make.
- Letting AI reformat a messy spreadsheet → then spot-checking calculations before you act.

Keeping Perspective

The people who get the most out of AI aren't the ones who use it for everything — they're the ones who know *when not to use it.* They see it as a force multiplier, not a replacement. They understand its patterns and blind spots.

And here's the part most overlooked: the better *you* get at your craft, the more valuable AI becomes. If you don't know what good marketing copy looks like, AI's draft won't magically fix that. If you can already recognize strong copy, AI becomes a way to produce more of it in less time.

Key Takeaways from This Chapter

- AI is a prediction engine, not a mind. It's powerful, but it doesn't "understand" like you do.

- It excels at summarizing, generating drafts, and recognizing patterns.
- It fails when accuracy, nuance, or ethical judgment are critical — unless you guide it.
- Your role is to set direction, verify results, and inject the human context AI can't produce.

If you hold on to those principles, you'll avoid the trap of overhyping AI or underestimating it. You'll see it for what it is — a tool you can shape to fit your work, rather than the other way around.

CHAPTER 2

Models in Practice: Capabilities, Constraints, and Cost

Getting Started with AI Artificial intelligence (If you're going to work with AI in any meaningful way, you need to understand the playing field. Not just the brand names or flashy demos — but how the different types of models work, where they perform best, and what limitations you'll run into.

This isn't about turning you into a machine learning engineer. It's about giving you the working knowledge to pick the right tool for the job, avoid paying for features you don't need, and plan around the quirks of these systems.

Types of AI Models You'll Encounter

AI isn't one thing. It's a whole stack of models built for different purposes. Knowing the categories makes it easier to choose without getting lost in marketing terms.

Large Language Models (LLMs)

These are text-based models trained to predict words in sequence. That means they can write, summarize, answer questions, and even code — if the request can be framed as text.

Examples:

- **OpenAI's GPT-4 / GPT-4o** – General-purpose, strong reasoning abilities.
- **Anthropic's Claude** – Longer context window, often better at concise summaries.
- **Google's Gemini** – Integrated into search and productivity tools.

Strengths: drafting content, answering structured queries, and providing explanations.

Weaknesses: accuracy drops on niche or up-to-the-minute topics without connected data.

Multimodal Models

These handle more than one type of input and output — for example, text plus images, or audio plus video.

Examples:

- **GPT-5** – Can interpret images, diagrams, and screenshots alongside text.
- **Gemini Pro Vision** – Image understanding with context-rich text generation.
- **Midjourney / DALL·E** – Text-to-image generation.

Strengths: creative work, design feedback, product mockups.

Weaknesses: more resource-heavy, higher cost per request.

Domain-Specific Models

These are trained for specific industries or tasks, such as legal research, medical imaging, and code analysis. They often outperform general-purpose models in their niche.

Examples:

- **Harvey AI** – Law-specific research.
- **Pictory AI** – Video summarization and editing.
- **Codex** – Code generation and debugging.

Strengths: higher accuracy in the domain they're tuned for. Weaknesses: less flexible outside their specialty.

Fine-Tuned Models

Sometimes, companies take a general model and fine-tune it with their data — making it more effective for a specific tone, style, or problem set.

Example: A retail brand fine-tuning a model to match its voice in customer service responses.

Strengths: consistent output in your brand or workflow. Weaknesses: requires setup and ongoing data updates.

Closed vs. Open-Source Tools

When you start exploring AI, you'll notice a split: some tools are "closed" (you only get what the company gives you), and some are "open-source" (you can access the model weights, run it yourself, or customize it).

Closed Models

These are like renting a fully furnished apartment. You get the keys, everything works, but you can't knock down walls or replace the furniture.

Examples: ChatGPT, Claude, Gemini.

Pros:

- Easy to start using.
- Hosted and maintained for you.
- Often higher polish in UI and integrations.

Cons:

- You're locked into their features and pricing.
- Less control over data privacy (though many have enterprise options).

Open-Source Models

These are like building your own space from the ground up. You can run them locally or on your server, tweak them, and integrate them however you want.

Pros:

- Complete control and customization.
- It can be cheaper in the long term for high-volume use.
- No vendor lock-in.

Cons:

- Requires technical know-how to set up and maintain.

- May lag top closed models in specific capabilities.

Which Should You Use?

If you're just getting started, closed models are the fastest way to get real work done. As your needs grow — especially if privacy, control, or custom workflows are important — open-source becomes more appealing.

Understanding Context Windows

The "context window" is the amount of information a model can consider in one go. Think of it as the size of the whiteboard it has in front of it.

- **Small context (e.g., 4K tokens)** – Good for short conversations or single documents.
- **Medium context (e.g., 32K tokens)** – Can handle a few long documents or a detailed back-and-forth.
- **Large context (e.g., 200K+ tokens)** – Can read an entire book or multi day meeting transcripts before responding.

The catch? Larger context models often incur higher costs per request and may be slower. And just because a model can "remember" more at once doesn't mean it uses that memory perfectly — it may still miss details buried in the middle.

Latency: Why Speed Varies

Latency refers to the delay between sending a request and receiving a response. It's affected by:

- **Model size** – Bigger brains take longer to think.

- **Server load** – More users = slower responses.
- **Your internet connection** – Sometimes it's just you.

For real-time or customer-facing applications (such as chatbots and live translation), latency is crucial. For research or writing tasks, a few extra seconds isn't a big deal — as long as the quality's worth the wait.

Pricing: What You're Paying For

AI pricing can be confusing because it's usually tied to tokens, not words. A "token" is a chunk of text — think of it like syllables.

- One thousand tokens equals 750 words in English.
- Most platforms charge per 1,000 tokens for both input and output.
- Some have flat monthly fees with usage caps.

Example: If your request is 500 words and the model generates 1,000 words, that's roughly 2,000 tokens you're billed for.

Cost Tips

1. **Batch work** – Group similar prompts in one request to reduce setup costs.
2. **Use smaller models for simpler tasks** – No need to call the most expensive model for a product title list.
3. **Watch the output length** – Overly verbose responses can eat your budget.

Matching the Right Model to the Job

When choosing an AI tool, pick one that plays to its strengths. Here are some practical examples:

- **Writing Marketing Copy** – Best Choice: GPT-4 or Claude. Why: Both have a strong natural language flow, producing persuasive, human-like copy with minimal editing.
- **Data Extraction** – Best Choice: Open-source fine-tuned models. Why: They're cheaper to run at scale and can be trained for repeatable, structured results.
- **Creative Image Generation** – Best Choice: Midjourney or DALL·E Why: Both specialize in high-quality visuals and can produce detailed, market-ready artwork from text prompts.
- **Coding Help** – Best Choice: GPT-4 Turbo or Codex Why: Excellent reasoning skills and the ability to maintain context across complex code discussions.
- **Customer Support Automation** – Best Choice: Fine-tuned LLaMA. Why: Can be trained privately to match your company's tone and handle sensitive customer interactions securely.

Avoiding Feature Overload

It's easy to think you need every new AI feature as soon as it launches. You don't. Chasing every tool can burn more time than it saves.

A better approach:

- Start with 1–2 models that cover 80% of your work.
- Only add more when you have a clear, repeatable need they solve.
- Keep notes on where your current tools fall short — those gaps guide your upgrades.

The Takeaway

Choosing the right AI model isn't about chasing the "most advanced" — it's about matching the model's strengths to the job at hand. Closed tools are excellent for speed and polish, while open-source tools offer control and customization. Context windows, latency, and pricing all factor into whether a model is practical for your workflow.

Get these fundamentals right, and you'll save time, money, and a lot of frustration down the road.

If you're ready, in the next chapter, we'll get into "Prompting That Survives Version Changes" — showing you how to write prompts that keep working even as the AI models evolve.

BONUS

The State of AI today: GPT-5, Claude 4, Gemini, Mistral & More

You've seen how AI models differ by capability, cost, and context in the last chapter. Here's a timely snapshot of where the AI frontier stands — because by the time your paperback hits shelves, this will still be relevant yearly.

Why This Chapter Matters

AI isn't a static field. Models are launching so fast that a reader picking up your book six months later might feel behind. By laying out the current landscape, you show readers you're informed and up to date, help them pick available tools, and anchor your workflows to real capabilities, not outdated assumptions. Let's look at what's out there — and what might work best for them.

You also need to decide how to use AI effectively. Should you stick with a single tool, or is it better to use the best of breed for your specific use case?

Major Players of Mid-2025

ChatGPT-5 (OpenAI)

Launched August 2025. Unifies several internal models into one "smart" system that automatically picks between fast answers and deep reasoning. Lower hallucination rates — ~45% less than GPT-4o, ~80% less than earlier model versions. Extended context windows — up to hundreds of thousands of tokens (API). Best-in-class coding, math, reasoning, and health performance.

Multi-mode access: GPT-5-mini, GPT-5-nano, plus GPT-5-pro ("Thinking mode"). Innovative router system for choosing reasoning level and even tone variants ("vibe coding"). Mixed user feedback — great for technical tasks, less engaging for creative tone; GPT-4o still sticks around. Platform integrations with Gmail, Teams, GitHub, and built-in access for Pro users

Claude Sonnet 4 (Anthropic)

Named Sonnet or Haiku, depending on version, optimized for speed, cost-efficiency, and ethical reasoning. Strong at long-form conversations with huge context windows — ideal for long inputs or regulatory workflows.

Gemini (Google)

Tight integration with the Google ecosystem; built for multimodal workflows and large-document understanding (millions of tokens)

Mistral

It's a new French startup, but take a look and compare it to ChatGPT. Lean, fast, cost-effective — ideal for high-volume or latency-sensitive workflows, especially if data sovereignty is a concern.

Smarter Choices Without Chasing Models

Pick workflows, not versions. On-ramp your prompts so they're easy to switch models — instead of rewriting everything when a model updates.

Layer with APIs, not a single model. GPT-5's reasoning mode, or context-heavy inputs via Gemini — choose dynamically based on task.

Let performance guide your model choice. If speed or cost is an issue, a learner, such as Claude or Mistral, may outdo GPT-5 even if it's newer.

"Pick Your Model" Exercise

Start with your most common task: blog posts, client emails, product descriptions?

Rank your needs: creative tone? Reasoning? Budget? Long context?

Test it now: run a prompt in all of them, try the same prompt in ChatGPT-5, Claude, Gemini, and follow up on the result — "Would this work well in my workflow long-term?"

Mark it as your go-to, then review again later if something better appears.

ChatGPT-5 has raised the baseline. It's faster, more accurate, and wiser than before — but it's still just a model. Your real edge is how you use it, not which version you're on. Build flexible systems, test often, and you'll stay ahead, no matter what drops next month.

When it comes to complex reasoning and coding, ChatGPT-5 is still the standout, excelling in benchmarks, debugging, and agentic-style tools. For low-cost bulk content or rapid testing, Mistral or Claude Haiku are ideal thanks to their speed and efficiency. If your work involves large documents or long-form projects, Gemini or Claude shine with their massive context windows and stability over lengthy inputs. For ethical or sensitive conversations, Claude is the safer choice, with a proven track record for restraint and compliance-friendly tone. For multimodal tasks that involve handling both video and documents, GPT-5 or Gemini offers the strongest built-in support.

CHAPTER 3

Prompting That Survives Version Changes

One of the most frustrating things about working with AI is discovering that your go-to prompt stopped working the way it used to. You open the same file, run the same request, and the output feels… off. Sometimes it's subtle — the tone shifts. Other times, it's as if the model has forgotten what you meant entirely.

This isn't because the AI is "broken." It's because models evolve. They get new training data, different parameters, or updated moderation rules. If your prompts are fragile, they'll crumble under those changes. If they're built well, they'll survive.

Let's talk about how to build prompts that keep working no matter what the model looks like next month.

O – Optimize with AI

This is the O in PROMPT: Optimize with AI. Raw outputs are rarely ready to use. Your edge comes from rewriting, re-prompting, and polishing until the AI's work matches your goal. Think of it as training the model on your style in real time.

Why Version Changes Break Prompts

AI models, huge language models (LLMs), are prediction machines. They decide what word comes next based on patterns in their training data and your input.

When a model is updated:

- **Training data changes** – New examples shift what the model considers "normal."
- **System behavior changes** – Developers tweak how it interprets instructions.
- **Bias handling changes** – The model may refuse specific requests that it previously answered.

If your prompt relies on quirks of the current version — like knowing it tends to start answers a certain way — it's vulnerable.

Structuring Prompts for Consistency

Think of a prompt like a recipe. If you say "make pasta," you're leaving a lot to chance — type of pasta, sauce, cooking method. But if you give a clear set of instructions, you're more likely to get the result you expect.

A durable prompt usually includes:

1. **Role** – Who or what the AI should act as.
2. **Objective** – The specific task you want completed.
3. **Constraints** – Any rules, limits, or exclusions.
4. **Format** – How the output should be structured.

5. **Example(s)** – A model of what you consider sound output.

Example: Fragile vs. Durable Prompt

Fragile:

Write a blog post about coffee.

Durable:

You are a specialty coffee roaster writing for a beginner audience.
Write a 600-word blog post explaining how to choose coffee beans for home brewing.

Use a friendly, conversational tone and three section headings. Avoid industry jargon and keep each paragraph under five sentences.
Example of desired tone: "Great coffee isn't complicated — it's just about knowing what you like."

The durable version sets role, audience, tone, length, and structure — making it less sensitive to model drift.

Using Roles, Constraints, and Examples

These three elements are your stability anchors.

Roles

When you tell the AI who it's supposed to be, you frame its style, perspective, and vocabulary.

- "Act as a financial advisor for young entrepreneurs."
- "You are a project manager coaching a remote team."

Roles help the AI filter its knowledge through a specific lens.

Constraints

Constraints keep the model from wandering. They're like guardrails on a road — without them, the AI might drift into unrelated territory.

- Word count limits.
- Banned phrases.
- Required section headings.
- Specific formats (tables, bullet lists, step-by-step).

Examples

A good example is worth a paragraph of instructions. If you can show the AI what you want, you reduce ambiguity.

- Paste a short example of tone or format before your request.
- If giving multiple examples, label them so the AI understands which is which.

Adapting Prompts Across Model Updates

When a model changes, don't throw out your entire prompt library. Instead, treat it like software that needs occasional updates.

Keep a Prompt Log

Document your best prompts along with:

- Model used.

- Date tested.
- Notes on output quality.

That way, if an update changes behavior, you have a baseline to compare against.

Test on Multiple Models

If your prompt only works on one model, it's brittle. Run it on at least two — even if you don't use the second one regularly. This forces you to write in a way that's less dependent on quirks.

Use Fallback Variants

Have a "lite" version of your prompt that's shorter and stripped of extras. If a model starts rejecting your detailed prompt, the lite version might still get the job done.

Re-evaluate Constraints Periodically

Some constraints become unnecessary as models improve. Others need tightening. For example, a model might get better at summarization so that you can remove sentence-by-sentence instructions — but worse at sticking to tone, so you add more examples.

When to Use Step-by-Step Prompts

One way to stabilize results is to have the AI work in steps instead of trying to do everything at once. This approach works across versions because it reduces the complexity of each request.

Example:

1. Ask for an outline first.

2. Approve or tweak it.
3. Have the AI expand each section.

This "multi-pass" method keeps control in your hands and limits the risk of a single bad output ruining the whole task.

Prompt Patterns That Tend to Last

From working across multiple model updates, a few patterns consistently hold up:

- **Instruction → Example → Task**
- **Role → Task → Constraints → Output format**
- **Ask for reasoning before the answer** (helps avoid hallucinations)

Prompt Pattern:

Role: You are a customer support trainer.

Task: Create a training script for handling late-delivery complaints.

Constraints: Keep it under 500 words. Include three bullet points for "Key Phrases to Use." Avoid apologizing more than twice.

Example: "We understand how frustrating this must be for you. Let's work together to fix it."

Output: Present as a numbered script with stage directions in brackets.

Why Over-Engineering Prompts Can Backfire

It's tempting to pack every detail into a prompt. But sometimes less is more. Over-engineered prompts can:

- Confuse the model.
- Increase costs (more tokens = more money).
- Break when the model changes its interpretation of a specific word or phrase.

A good rule: include just enough detail to guide the output, then refine in follow-up messages.

The Human Element Still Matters

No matter how durable your prompts are, they still require human judgment. You'll need to:

- Spot when tone or accuracy drifts.
- Determine whether constraints are beneficial or detrimental.
- Adapt prompts to new tools or use cases.

The most resilient prompt strategy is not about locking down one perfect version forever — it's about having a flexible process to test and adjust.

Your Prompt Survival Kit

If you want prompts that survive model changes, keep this checklist:

1. **Define the role** – Who is the AI in this task?

2. **State the objective clearly** – What's the exact goal?
3. **Add constraints** – Word count, tone, banned content.
4. **Provide an example** – Show, don't just tell.
5. **Specify output format** – Table, bullet list, script.
6. **Test on multiple models** – Check for portability.
7. **Version-control your prompts** – Keep notes on what works.

Key Takeaways

- AI updates are inevitable—prompts built on structure, not quirks, last longer.
- Roles, constraints, and examples give you stability anchors.
- Keep a prompt log, test across models, and have fallback versions ready.
- Avoid over-engineering — clarity beats complexity.
- Treat prompting as an evolving skill, not a one-time setup.

In the next chapter, we'll put these principles to work in Your First AI Workflow in 30 Minutes — walking through a complete mini-project from idea to output, with a prompt strategy that works today and still will next year.

CHAPTER 4

Your First AI Workflow in 30 Minutes

Reading about AI is one thing. Using it to get something done is where it clicks. You don't need weeks of study before you can make it work for you — you can complete a worthwhile project in less than half an hour.

This chapter will walk you through one quick-start mini-project from idea to output. You'll see the decisions to make along the way, the prompts to use, and how to evaluate what you get back so you can improve it.

The goal isn't just to follow along. It's to show you the pattern you can apply to almost anything — content creation, research, customer support, planning — and get a working result fast.

The Project: Create a Short, Useful Guide

Let's say you run a small online store selling eco-friendly home products. You want a free downloadable PDF guide you can offer in exchange for email sign-ups — a "lead magnet" in marketing terms.

You decide the topic will be:

"5 Simple Ways to Make Your Kitchen More Sustainable."

That's our starting point. By the end of this workflow, you'll have a draft guide ready to format and share.

Define the End Goal (5 minutes)

Before you open ChatGPT, Claude, or any other AI tool, you need clarity. The more specific you are about your goal, the better your results.

Ask yourself:

- Who is this for? (Audience)
- What do I want them to know, feel, or do after reading? (Outcome)
- How will I measure if the result works? (Success criteria)

For our guide:

- **Audience:** Busy homeowners who care about reducing waste but don't want complicated projects.
- **Outcome:** Give them five practical, low-cost tips they can start this week.
- **Success:** People download it, join the email list, and a portion eventually buy products from the store.

Choose the Right Model (2 minutes)

For this job, any modern LLM (Large Language Model) works — GPT-4, Claude, Gemini — because it's a short written piece for a general audience. You don't need a domain-specific or open-source model here.

If speed and cost matter more than maximum nuance, you could even use a cheaper "turbo" variant.

Build the Core Prompt (5 minutes)

You could type "write a guide about sustainable kitchens" and hope for the best. However, we want a durable and precise prompt that yields something close to final-draft quality.

Prompt: You are a sustainability expert writing for busy homeowners who want practical, eco-friendly tips.

Write a 750-word guide titled "5 Simple Ways to Make Your Kitchen More Sustainable."

Each tip should have a clear heading, a short explanation, and 1–2 actionable steps.

Keep the tone friendly and encouraging, avoiding technical jargon, and ensure each tip is low-cost to implement. Format as numbered sections with bold headings.

This prompt gives role, audience, objective, constraints, and format — all in one shot.

Generate and Review the First Draft (5 minutes)

You run the prompt and get back a neatly structured guide. The tips are solid, but two of them feel too generic ("Use Energy-Efficient Appliances" could use more detail).

Instead of rewriting manually, we'll have the AI improve itself.

Follow-up **Prompt:** In Tip #2, add specific examples of low-cost energy-efficient appliances under $50. In Tip #4, suggest two homemade alternatives to store-bought cleaning products. Keep the rest as is.

This refinement stage is where you save the most time. You're acting like an editor giving notes, not a ghostwriter doing the heavy lifting.

Add Extra Value (5 minutes)

Good outputs become great when you add something that sets them apart — a chart, checklist, or quick reference table. AI can produce these in seconds.

Prompt: Add a one-page checklist version of these tips at the end of the guide so readers can print it and put it on their fridge.

Now your lead magnet has two formats in one: the complete guide and a quick-scan version.

Evaluate Before You Publish (3 minutes)

Don't assume the AI got everything right. Your evaluation has two jobs:

1. Check for factual accuracy and practicality.
2. Make sure the tone matches your brand.

For factual checks:

- Are the recommended products or tips realistic?
- Is the pricing accurate?
- Do any claims need citations?

For tone checks:

- Does it sound like something *you* would say?
- Does it speak to your audience without talking down to them?

If something feels off, consider running another refinement prompt. Adjust the tone to be slightly more upbeat and add a short intro paragraph inviting readers to take action this week.

Prepare for Re-use (5 minutes)

You don't want to rebuild this prompt from scratch every time you need a similar project. Save it in a "Prompt Library" with variables you can swap in.

Template:

You are a [role] writing for [audience]. Write a [word count] guide titled "[title]." Each section should have [structure].

Keep the tone [tone] and avoid [exclusions]. Format as [output format].

Now you can use this to create "5 Simple Ways to…" guides for other rooms, topics, or products.

Workflow Recap

Here's the 30-minute timeline you just followed:

- **5 min** – Define end goal and audience.
- **2 min** – Choose model.
- **5 min** – Build core prompt.

- **5 min** – Generate and refine first draft.
- **5 min** – Add extra value elements.
- **3 min** – Evaluate for accuracy and tone.
- **5 min** – Save as reusable template.

This isn't just a one-off process — it's a pattern. Once you've done it once, you can adapt it for almost any short project.

How to Improve Results Over Time

Even with a strong prompt and process, your first try might only be "good enough." The real advantage comes when you learn from each run and feed those lessons back in.

Ways to improve:

- **Track feedback** from real readers — what they liked, what they ignored.
- **Iterate on structure** — maybe a future guide works better as a Q&A format.
- **Add media** — combine AI text with AI-generated images for a stronger visual appeal.

What This Teaches You About AI Productivity

1. **Speed doesn't mean sloppy.** You can get a usable draft fast if you define it well.
2. **The AI is your assistant, not your replacement.** You guide, it executes.
3. **Small improvements compound.** Adding a checklist took less than a minute but doubled the guide's usefulness.

4. **Reusable templates save time.** The second project will be even faster than the first.

Next Steps for You

Don't just read this chapter — run it. Pick a mini-project that's useful to you right now:

- A FAQ for your website.
- A "Top 10 Tips" sheet for customers.
- A short guide for your social media followers.

Block out 30 minutes, follow the steps, and you'll have something tangible by the end.

The first time you do this, you'll be amazed at how much you can get done in a short session. The second time, you'll realize the real magic is in the pattern — and that pattern is now yours to apply anywhere.

In the next chapter, we'll move from quick wins to **core AI workflows** that deliver ongoing value — research assistants, content engines, and other repeatable systems you can run day after day.

PART II

Core Workflows: From Idea to Execution

Now that you've got the foundations down, it's time to put AI to work. Part II is about the real workflows—the day-to-day engines that turn ideas into content, services, and systems. Think of this section as your "AI toolbox in action." Each chapter gives you a mode, a repeatable way to use AI to save time and create value.

- **Chapter 5** puts AI into *Research Assistant Mode*, helping you uncover insights, trends, and opportunities without drowning in tabs.
- **Chapter 6** is *Content Engine Mode*, showing how AI can crank out drafts, posts, and campaigns that would take hours to do by hand.
- **Chapter 7** takes AI into *Inbox and Meetings Mode*, reducing email chaos and helping you walk into meetings prepared instead of overwhelmed.
- **Chapter 8** covers *Small-Biz Operations Mode*, where AI keeps the boring admin off your plate so you can focus on the money work.

- **Chapter 9** focuses on *Data Extraction and Cleanup Mode*, which sounds technical but can be a game-changer when you're dealing with messy spreadsheets or customer lists.

- **Chapter 10** closes the section with *Planning and Decision Support Mode*, where AI acts like a second brain for strategy and problem-solving.

This is where the **R** in **PROMPT—Research Winning Content—comes alive.** Most people use AI as a task finisher: "write this blog post," "draft this email." That's fine, but it's not where the real edge is. The edge is in research. AI can scan thousands of reviews, pull themes from transcripts, summarize competitor strategies, or spot gaps in what's trending. That's not busywork—it's intelligence.

The workflows in Part II all build on this research power. Chapter 5 shows it directly, but even in Chapter 7 (Inbox and Meetings Mode), research is the hidden weapon. AI doesn't just answer—it prepares you. It helps you walk into conversations with facts, not guesses. It enables you to notice what matters before anyone else does.

Treat AI as your research partner, not just your writing partner, and you'll see opportunities where others see noise. That's why R is threaded through this section—it's the engine that makes every workflow sharper and more profitable.

CHAPTER 5

Research Assistant Mode

When people first discover AI, one of the most tempting uses is to have it "look things up" for them. And while AI can feel like an all-knowing expert, it's not a search engine. It's a pattern recognition system that generates text based on the data it's seen. That means it can be brilliant for specific research tasks — and completely unreliable for others.

R – Research Winning Content

This is the R in the PROMPT Goldmine System™: Research Winning Content. ChatGPT can pull patterns out of Amazon reviews, YouTube transcripts, Reddit threads, and more. Use it to reverse-engineer what's already winning in your space.

If you understand what it can and can't do in this mode, you'll save yourself a lot of frustration. More importantly, you'll learn how to set it up as a genuine research assistant — one that finds, organizes, and explains information in a way that's useful to you.

What "Research Assistant Mode" Really Means

Research Assistant Mode isn't a switch you flip in the interface. It's a way of using an AI model with a straightforward process:

1. **Frame a question** in a way that fits the AI's strengths.
2. **Break the task into parts** so each step builds on the last.
3. **Cross-check the results** with reliable sources.

Think of it like having an eager intern: if you say, "Go find me everything about climate change," you'll get a messy dump of information. But if you say, "Find three credible sources that explain how climate change affects coastal cities, then summarize each in under 200 words," you'll get something structured you can use.

When AI Shines in Research

Some tasks play directly to the AI's strengths:

- **Summarizing long text** – Give it a research paper, meeting transcript, or article, and it can distill the main points quickly.
- **Structuring messy information** – It can turn scattered notes into a clear outline.
- **Explaining complex ideas in plain language** – Great for when you understand the basics but need it in simpler terms for others.
- **Brainstorming possible angles** – For example, listing potential causes of a trend before you dig deeper into each one.

Where AI Fails (and Why)

AI doesn't "know" things. It generates what looks like knowledge. This can lead to:

- **Hallucinations** – Confidently stating false information.
- **Outdated facts** – If the model was last trained two years ago, it won't know about last week's news unless connected to a live data source.
- **Missing citations** – Or worse, fabricating them.

The takeaway: never use AI research output as your only source of truth. Use it to shape and speed up your process, not to replace real verification.

Setting Up for Fact-Checking and Data Gathering

Let's walk through a safe research workflow you can run in any general-purpose LLM.

Define the Question Clearly

Bad: Tell me about electric cars.

Better: Provide a summary of the three most common battery technologies used in electric vehicles in 2024. For each, list the advantages, disadvantages, and two major manufacturers using it.

This approach:

- Narrows the topic.
- Defines the number of items.
- Specifies the structure.

Ask for the Structure First

Before getting content, ask the model to suggest an outline for the answer. This gives you a chance to correct any misunderstandings.

Prompt: Create an outline for a 1,000-word briefing on current battery technologies in electric vehicles, aimed at non-technical readers.

Gather the Raw Material

Once you approve the outline, have the AI fill in each section — but tell it to flag anything it's not sure about.

Prompt: Expand section 1 using only facts you are confident in. If you're unsure, note "requires verification."

This is how you avoid quietly absorbing bad information.

Verify Externally

If the AI mentions "Lithium-sulfur batteries are now used by Tesla," don't take that at face value. Search trusted sources (company press releases, reputable news outlets, industry reports) to confirm.

Summarizing Without Losing the Point

A good research assistant doesn't just copy and paste — it distills. Here's a reliable prompt pattern for summaries:

Summarize the following article in under 200 words for a [target audience]. Include the main argument, 2–3 key supporting points, and any notable statistics. Exclude minor details.

This works because it:

- Defines length.
- Name the audience.
- Sets the summary focus.

Turning Dense Text into Actionable Insights

Original paragraph from a climate report:

"Global sea levels have risen approximately 8–9 inches (21–24 cm) since 1880, with about a third of that rise occurring in the last two and a half decades. The acceleration is largely attributed to increased melting of glaciers and ice sheets, coupled with thermal expansion of seawater as it warms. This trend poses significant threats to coastal cities, including more frequent flooding, loss of habitat, and saltwater intrusion into freshwater supplies."

AI Summary Prompt Output:

Sea levels have risen 8–9 inches since 1880, with one-third of the increase in just the past 25 years. This is due to the melting of ice and the warming of oceans. Coastal cities face higher flood risks, habitat loss, and saltwater contamination of freshwater sources.

Result: Same meaning, less jargon, faster to digest.

Avoiding Hallucinations

Hallucinations happen when the model tries to "fill in the blanks" with plausible but false details. To reduce the risk:

1. **Ask for uncertainty markers** – Tell it to flag where confidence is low.
2. **Request sources** – Even if you know they might be incomplete, they guide your verification.
3. **Break down the task** – Smaller chunks mean fewer opportunities for fabrication.

Hallucination Trap Example

You ask: Who invented the Internet?

An AI might confidently name "Sir Tim Berners-Lee," which is wrong for "internet" (he created the World Wide Web). This happens because the model conflates similar concepts.

Fix: Provide a brief history of the development of the Internet. Name key individuals and their specific contributions. If uncertain about a detail, note it.

Practical Example: Competitor Research in Business

Let's say you run a boutique coffee roasting business and want to understand competitors' marketing approaches.

Workflow:

1. **Ask for a structured comparison** – List five direct-to-consumer coffee brands. For each, summarize their main value proposition, pricing range, and marketing tone.
2. **Have AI create a comparison table** - organize information into a table format so you can easily compare multiple options side by side.
3. **Spot-check each brand's website** – Verify details and note anything the AI missed.

Result: You save hours identifying trends without relying on the AI as your only source.

Why Iteration Beats One-and-Done Requests

The difference between a mediocre and an excellent AI research session is iteration. Instead of dumping your question in once, treat it as a back-and-forth:

- **Clarify** – Get the AI to rephrase your question before answering.
- **Drill down** – Ask for details on just one section.
- **Reframe** – Change the angle if results feel shallow.

This mimics how you'd work with a real assistant — you wouldn't accept their first draft without adjustments.

Key Prompt Templates for Research Mode

- **For outlines:** Propose an outline for [topic], aimed at [audience], focusing on [specific angle].
- **For summaries:** Summarize [source/text] in under [word count], including [specific elements] and excluding [irrelevant details].
- **For fact-check prep:** Provide a list of claims about [topic] that require verification from external sources.
- **For comparison tables:** Create a table comparing [X items] by [criteria].

The Human Role in AI Research

AI can organize and accelerate the messy middle of research, but the critical thinking is yours:

- You decide what's worth asking.
- You interpret the results.
- You verify accuracy before acting.

If you skip that last step, you're not doing research — you're gambling.

Takeaways

- AI in research mode is a multiplier, not a replacement.
- Structure and clarity in your prompts make results far more helpful.
- Always verify important facts externally.
- Utilize iteration and break tasks into manageable parts to enhance quality.
- Recognize when the AI is speculating — and treat those points as leads, not conclusions.

In the next chapter, we'll move from research into Content Engine Mode — using AI to produce consistent, high-quality material at scale without sounding robotic.

CHAPTER 6

Content Engine Mode

One of the most reliable ways to monetize AI is to turn it into a content engine. This repeatable system produces blog posts, social media updates, ad copy, and other material on demand. This isn't about spamming the internet with low-quality filler. It's about scaling your ability to produce high-value content without burning out.

When you set this up right, you can go from idea to publish-ready assets in hours instead of days — all while keeping your brand voice consistent and your audience engaged.

Why Content Still Drives Revenue

No matter how algorithms change, two truths hold:

1. People buy from brands they trust.
2. Content is how trust gets built at scale.

Good content draws attention, positions you as an authority, and keeps your audience coming back. It fuels SEO, social media reach, email engagement — and all of that eventually drives sales.

The problem? Quality content takes time. That's where AI comes in — not to replace you, but to multiply your output.

The Content Engine Mindset

You don't want to treat AI content creation as random bursts of inspiration. The key is to think like a media company:

- Topics and formats are planned — you're not waking up and guessing what to post.
- Templates guide production — no reinventing the wheel every time.
- Outputs are batched — multiple pieces are created in one session.

Core Content Types You Can Produce

Blog Posts

- SEO-focused evergreen guides.
- Industry commentary.
- Case studies.

Social Media Posts

- Short-form updates (X, LinkedIn).
- Carousel posts for Instagram.
- TikTok/short video scripts.

Ad Copy

- Facebook and Instagram ads.
- Google Search ads.
- Landing page headlines.

Building a Blog Post Workflow

AI can take you from topic idea to SEO-optimized draft in under an hour.

Generate topic ideas

Prompt: Act as an SEO strategist. Suggest 10 blog topics for [your niche] that have high search potential but low competition. Include a short description and target keyword for each.

Build an outline

Prompt: Create an outline for a 1,200-word blog post on "[topic]" targeting "[keyword]." Include 5–7 headings with short descriptions of what each section should cover.

Draft the post

Prompt: Using the approved outline, write the blog post in a conversational yet authoritative tone. Keep paragraphs under four sentences and include at least one statistic per main section.

Add meta elements

Prompt: Suggest an SEO title under 60 characters and a meta description under 160 characters for this blog post.

Social Media Content at Scale

The key to utilizing AI for social media is to batch-create posts and tailor them to each platform.

Example: Turning One Blog Post into Multiple Social Pieces

If your blog post is "10 Easy Indoor Plants for Beginners":

- Instagram carousel: 10 slides, one plant per slide.
- Twitter/X thread: Each tweet = a short plant tip.
- TikTok script: 60-second "Top 5" version.

Prompt: Turn this blog post into:

1 Instagram carousel script (title + text per slide),

1 Twitter thread (10 tweets), and

1 TikTok video script under 60 seconds. Keep the tone playful and beginner-friendly.

Ad Copy That Converts

AI excels at generating multiple ad variants, allowing you to test what works.

Prompt: Create five variations of Facebook ad copy for [product/service]. Each should have:

- A headline under 40 characters.
- Body text under 100 characters.
- A call to action encouraging purchase.

You can also feed it your best-performing past ads so it mimics your proven style.

Batch Content Creation Workflows

Batching is where the real productivity boost happens. Instead of doing idea → draft → edit → publish for one piece at a time, you do each stage for multiple pieces in one sitting.

Example Weekly Workflow:

- Monday: Brainstorm and outline five blog posts.
- Tuesday: Generate and refine first drafts for all 5.
- Wednesday: Repurpose into social media formats.
- Thursday: Create ad copy for related offers.
- Friday: Review, edit, and schedule everything.

Why Batching Works

- Reduces context switching — you're in "idea mode" or "writing mode," not both.
- AI can work faster when fed related prompts in sequence.
- You can queue weeks of content at once, freeing time for strategy.

Example: Content Engine for a Coaching Business

Goal: Increase leads for a life coaching service.

Monthly Batch Plan:

1. 4 long-form blog posts — Topics like productivity, work-life balance, and goal setting.
2. Daily social media posts — Quotes, short tips, and polls.

3. Bi-weekly email newsletter — Recaps best tips and invites to free webinars.

4. Ad campaigns — Promote coaching sessions using client testimonials.

AI will handle Topic ideation, drafting, and repurposing across formats.

The human will handle editing for brand tone, add personal stories, and approve the final schedule.

Avoiding the "AI Blandness" Trap

If you tell AI to "write a blog post," you'll get generic output. To keep it fresh:

- Feed it your brand voice guide.
- Include specific examples from your own experience.
- Add stats and references from verified sources.

Prompt: Rewrite this post in a more personal tone, adding two real-life examples and one counterpoint to keep the reader engaged.

Scaling Without Losing Quality

A strong content engine isn't about volume alone — it's about consistent quality.

- Set style standards — Length, formatting, voice.
- Track performance — Which posts drive traffic or sales? Feed that back into your prompts.

- Audit regularly — Remove outdated or underperforming content.

Your Content Engine Starter Kit

1. Core templates for blog posts, social posts, and ads.
2. Repurposing prompts to spin one asset into multiple formats.
3. A batching schedule that fits your workflow.
4. Metrics dashboard (could be as simple as a spreadsheet) to track what works.

AI can run a content engine that covers blogs, social media, and ads — but only if you set up a structured workflow.

Repurposing and batching multiply your results without multiplying your work hours.

Quality control is still human-led — AI speeds the work, but you make it resonate.

In the next chapter, we'll dig into **Inbox and Meeting Management Mode** — where AI becomes your assistant for communication, scheduling, and keeping projects on track.

CHAPTER 7

Inbox and Meetings Mode

For many people, email and meetings eat up more hours than actual work. AI can't take the calls for you (yet), but it can strip away the tedious parts — drafting replies, summarizing discussions, and keeping your notes in order. Used well, this turns your inbox and calendar from time sinks into controlled, low-effort systems.

R – Research Winning Content

Even here, the R—Research Winning Content—matters. Before a big meeting or client pitch, use AI to scan competitor websites or pull trends from industry news. Walk in with insights, not just opinions.

Drafting Email Replies

A simple but powerful use: feeding AI the incoming message and having it generate a draft reply.

Prompt: Draft a polite, concise reply to the following email. Please keep your message under 100 words and confirm the meeting for Thursday at 2 PM. [Paste email]

You can set tone guidelines ("friendly," "formal," "persuasive") so your responses match your style.

Pro tip: Never let the AI hit "send" without you. Review, tweak, and personalize before finalizing.

Summarizing Calls and Meetings

If you record or transcribe meetings, AI can turn messy notes into clean summaries.

Prompt: Summarize the following meeting transcript into:

- Main decisions made
- Action items (with owners)
- Key discussion points

This keeps the focus on outcomes rather than every word said. It also makes follow-ups clear, so nothing gets lost in a pile of "we should."

Auto-Scheduling Without Back-and-Forth

AI can draft scheduling proposals for you.

Prompt: Based on my availability (Monday–Thursday, 9 AM–2 PM CST), suggest three possible meeting times in the next week. Include time zone conversions for EST and PST.

When paired with tools like Calendly or Motion, AI can pre-fill details for invites, agendas, and reminders.

Keeping a Personal Knowledge Base Updated

Inbox and meeting data are only helpful if you can find them later. You can have AI summarize and file important messages or meeting notes into a personal knowledge base (Notion, Obsidian, Google Docs).

Workflow:

1. Forward key emails or transcripts to a dedicated folder.
2. Run a script or automation that sends them to AI for summarizing.
3. Store the summaries in your knowledge base with tags.

Over time, this becomes a searchable archive of decisions, client requests, and project history.

Why This Works

- **Context awareness** – AI can connect the dots between related conversations, providing a deeper understanding of the context.
- **Speed** – A good draft reply or summary takes seconds instead of minutes.
- **Memory** – Your knowledge base becomes the "extended brain" you can reference anytime.

Inbox and meeting management isn't glamorous, but it's where a lot of time gets wasted. AI helps by:

- Drafting first-pass responses.
- Turning raw transcripts into actionable notes.
- Suggesting schedules without endless email chains.
- Filing important info where you can find it later.

With the basics automated, you can spend less time on logistics and more on the work that moves the needle.

Next, we'll look at **Small-Biz Ops Mode** — where AI helps you run your entire back office with fewer moving parts.

CHAPTER 8

Small-Biz Operations Mode

Running a small business isn't just about selling your product or delivering your service. It's also about the endless "back office" work: invoices, proposals, CRM updates, customer service emails, scheduling, record-keeping. It's a lot of hats for one person — and if you're like most entrepreneurs, these operational tasks steal time and mental energy from your actual money-making work.

This is where AI can step in, not as a flashy novelty, but as the quiet, dependable workhorse that keeps your business running smoothly in the background.

Why Operations Deserve AI Attention

Marketing and sales get all the buzz, but smooth operations are what keep your business from collapsing under its weight. You can survive a bad marketing month. You can't survive chaos in billing, client communications, or customer service.

Small businesses often resist adopting systems because they feel they are restrictive. But here's the thing: the right systems create freedom. AI makes them faster to set up and cheaper to run.

Core Operational Areas AI Can Support

1. Invoicing and Payment Tracking
2. Client Proposals
3. CRM (Customer Relationship Management) Updates
4. Customer Service Responses
5. Internal Documentation
6. Basic Compliance and Record-Keeping

We'll walk through each area, with practical workflows and prompt examples you can drop into your tools.

Invoicing and Payment Tracking

Most invoicing software — like QuickBooks, FreshBooks, or Wave — already has templates. But AI can handle the repetitive, personalized parts: writing invoice descriptions, following up on late payments, and summarizing account status for you.

Example Prompt for Invoice Descriptions:

Write a one-sentence invoice description for [service/product] provided to [client name] on [date]. Keep it professional and clear.

You can also ask AI to:

- Generate polite late-payment reminders.
- Summarize monthly receivables so you see immediately who owes what.

When connected through automation tools (Zapier, Make), this can happen without you even opening your invoicing app.

Client Proposals

A proposal is often a mix of boilerplate and custom sections. The boilerplate is easy; the custom part — showing you understand the client's needs — is what takes time.

Proposal Workflow:

1. Feed AI a brief with client details, project scope, and any specific requests.
2. Have AI generate a first draft proposal in your preferred structure.
3. Review and add personal touches — case studies, portfolio samples.

Prompt: Draft a client proposal for [service] to [client], based on this scope: [paste scope]. Include introduction, proposed solution, timeline, and pricing.

You can store a "proposal template" prompt so that every time you need one, the structure is identical, and only the variables change.

CRM Updates

Keeping your CRM updated is the operational equivalent of flossing — everyone says they'll do it, but few do consistently.

AI can:

- Convert messy meeting notes into structured CRM entries.

- Generate follow-up email drafts based on the last client interaction.
- Suggest next steps for leads based on deal stage.

Example:

You paste in your scribbled meeting notes:

Met with Sam from BrightTech. Interested in the premium package but wants a discount. Said to follow up after budget review in 2 weeks."

AI turns that into:

- Lead: Sam Johnson – BrightTech
- Stage: Negotiation
- Following Action: Send updated proposal on April 15
- Notes: Wants discount; emphasize long-term ROI.

This keeps your pipeline clean and actionable, eliminating the need for hours of manual entry.

Customer Service with AI

AI can be your first line of customer support — not the final decision-maker, but the one answering the easy questions and routing the rest.

Tier 1: Quick Answers

For common questions ("What's your refund policy?"), AI can draft instant responses based on your policy documents.

Prompt: Based on this FAQ document, draft a response to: "Can I get a refund if I cancel after 10 days?"

Tier 2: Escalation

If the request is complex or emotional, AI can:

1. Draft a personalized empathy-first reply.

2. Flag it for human review before sending.

This speeds response times without risking brand damage from an automated tone-deaf answer.

Case Study: AI in a Boutique Design Studio

Before AI: Owner spent 3–4 hours weekly on invoicing, 2 hours drafting proposals, and endless time answering similar client emails.

After AI Implementation:

- AI-generated invoice descriptions and reminders saved 2+ hours/week
- Proposal drafts cut creation time by 50%.
- FAQ-based AI replies reduced client email volume by 30%.

Net result: More billable design hours, less admin.

Internal Documentation

If you ever train staff, hire freelancers, or need to recall how you did something six months ago, documentation is gold. AI can:

- Turn a recorded Loom video of you doing a process into a written SOP.
- Update existing docs with new screenshots or steps.
- Summarize tool settings so you can reconfigure quickly after changes.

Prompt: Turn this transcript into a step-by-step guide for onboarding a new client, with headings and bullet points for each stage.

Basic Compliance and Record-Keeping

While you should never rely on AI for legal compliance decisions, it can help you summarize compliance checklists in plain language, organize scanned receipts into categories, and generate reminders for filing deadlines.

Prompt: Based on this list of upcoming deadlines, create a 3-month calendar with reminders for each compliance task.

Automation Layer: Making It All Click

The real magic is connecting AI with your existing tools:

- **Zapier/Make**: Send meeting notes → AI → CRM.
- **Google Sheets + AI**: Auto-generate monthly financial summaries.
- **Gmail + AI**: Draft replies, then save them as templates.

This way, AI isn't another thing to manage — it's woven into your daily tools.

Where AI Won't Replace You

AI can't:

- Negotiate in nuanced client conversations.
- Decide which clients are worth pursuing.
- Catch every subtle error in a proposal.
- Maintain long-term relationships for you.

It's an accelerator, not a decision-maker.

AI can automate 60–70% of small-biz operations without losing quality.

Invoicing, proposals, CRM updates, and basic customer service are low-risk, high-reward areas to focus on initially.

The most significant gains come from automation + AI, not AI alone.

Keep human oversight for anything involving judgment, emotion, or legal compliance.

In the next chapter, we'll cover **Data Extraction and Cleanup Mode**— how to use AI to take raw, messy information and turn it into organized, actionable data you can use.

CHAPTER 9

Data Extraction and Cleanup Mode

Every business runs on data — but in the real world, that data is rarely neat. It's scattered across emails, PDFs, messy spreadsheets, and half-complete forms. You can't make wise decisions if your information is buried in chaos.

This is where AI becomes your quiet analyst. It's not about replacing your spreadsheet software or BI tools — it's about giving you a fast, flexible way to pull data out of the mess and into a usable format. When paired with automation, it can clean, organize, and even visualize information before you've finished your coffee.

Why This Matters

If you've ever wasted an afternoon manually cleaning a CSV file — deleting blank rows, fixing broken dates, converting currencies — you know that "data cleanup" can feel like punishment. And yet, this step is essential. Insufficient data leads to bad decisions. AI can cut the grunt work down from hours to minutes, leaving you with a dataset you can trust.

Where AI Fits in the Process

Think of data cleanup as a pipeline:

1. **Extraction** – Pulling data out of its original format (PDF, email, screenshot, form).

2. **Structuring** – Turning it into a table, list, or standardized format.

3. **Cleaning** – Removing duplicates, filling missing fields, fixing inconsistencies.

4. **Enrichment** – Adding missing details from other sources.

5. **Visualization** – Creating quick dashboards to spot trends.

AI can assist at every stage — either directly or by generating scripts and formulas for your existing tools.

Turning Messy Data into Tables

Let's say you have a list of customer orders copied from emails. Each entry is formatted differently:

John Smith – ordered 3x "Eco Water Bottle" for $75 – shipped 5/12

Eco Hoodie (Blue, Large), two pcs, $49.99 each – Sarah Lee – Delivered May 7

You can paste this into an AI and **Prompt**: Convert the following unstructured order list into a table with columns: Customer Name, Product, Quantity, Price Per Unit, Total, Status, Date.

From there, you can paste it directly into Excel or Google Sheets.

Cleaning Inconsistent Data

Real-world data is messy because humans enter it. Some people type "Yes," others "Y," and a few "Sure." That's a nightmare for filtering. AI can normalize these entries in bulk.

Prompt: Standardize all "yes" responses in column C to exactly "Yes." Replace all variations of "no" with "No." Leave blank cells unchanged.

For numbers, you can convert currencies, standardize date formats, and remove extra spaces or text.

Deduplication Without Headaches

Duplicate entries are another silent killer of data accuracy. AI can spot subtle duplicates — like "John Smith" and "Smith, John" — and merge them correctly.

Prompt: Identify and merge duplicate entries in this customer list. Use email addresses as the primary match and phone numbers as a secondary match.

Filling in the Gaps

AI can also enrich your data by pulling missing details from other sources. You have a list of business names without websites.

Prompt: For each business name in this list, search online and return the official website URL. If not found, return "Not Available."

If your AI tool has a web-connected mode, this can be done in one go. If not, it can still create a ready-to-use search list for a VA to complete.

Building Quick Dashboards

Once your data is clean, you want to see patterns — sales by region, top-performing products, response times. AI can help here in two ways: first, by generating chart-ready data — grouping, summing, calculating. And suggesting visual layouts — telling you which charts would best represent your data.

Prompt: From this cleaned sales data, create a summary table showing: Total sales per product, average order value, and total revenue by month. Suggest three chart types to visualize this.

Example: From Raw Export to Dashboard in One Hour

Scenario: You export a CSV from your e-commerce platform. It's 3,000 rows of orders, with inconsistent product names, blank shipping dates, and a dozen columns you don't need.

Workflow:

1. Ask AI to remove irrelevant columns (internal IDs, unused tags).
2. Standardize product names based on a master list.
3. Fill missing shipping dates by adding the order dates and the average processing time.
4. Group and sum orders by product for a monthly sales table.
5. Paste results into Google Data Studio or Excel to create charts.

Instead of spending 4–5 hours cleaning before analysis, you're done in under an hour.

Advanced Tip: AI-Generated Formulas and Scripts

Even if you prefer working in Excel or Google Sheets, AI can still speed things up by writing the exact formula or macro you need.

Prompt: Write a Google Sheets formula that extracts the domain name from an email address in column B.

Or: Write a Python script to merge these two CSV files on the "Customer ID" column and output a cleaned version without duplicates.

This combines AI's language skills with traditional data tools, letting you scale up without hiring a full-time analyst.

What About Accuracy?

Data cleanup AI is only as good as your instructions. If you don't define the format, it will make assumptions — and assumptions cause errors.

Rules for safer cleanup:

- Always specify column names and formats.
- Run a small test before processing the full dataset.
- Keep the raw data separate so you can roll back changes.

Case Study: Local Retailer's Sales Data Overhaul

A small home décor store had 18 months of sales spread across POS exports, supplier invoices, and handwritten notes. They needed to know which products were worth reordering.

With AI:

- All data sources were converted into a single spreadsheet with standardized columns.
- Missing categories were filled in.
- Sales were grouped by product type and season.

Outcome: They discovered that 70% of revenue came from just 15% of products. This insight drove smarter ordering and reduced dead stock.

Automation: The Next Level

You can combine AI with automation tools to make data cleanup part of your regular workflow:

- **Zapier/Make**: Every time a new CSV is dropped into Google Drive, send it through AI for cleaning and formatting.
- **Notion/Sheets Integration**: Auto-update dashboards when cleaned data is ready.

Where AI Won't Replace You

AI can't decide which metrics matter for your business. It can prepare the numbers — but you choose the story they tell. Human judgment is what turns clean data into valuable insights.

Messy data costs time and accuracy. AI can reduce cleanup time by 70–90%. Always define formats clearly to avoid costly errors. Use AI for extraction, structuring, cleaning, enrichment, and dashboard prep. Pair with automation tools for ongoing cleanup without manual effort.

Next, we'll get into **Planning and Decision Support Mode** — where AI stops just organizing your data and starts helping you decide what to do with it.

CHAPTER 10

Planning and Decision Support Mode

Running a business — or even managing your projects — is a constant cycle of deciding what to do next. Sometimes the right path is obvious; other times, you're weighing multiple options without enough information to feel confident. The bigger the stakes, the more you need clarity before moving forward.

AI isn't here to make your decisions for you. But it can become a structured thinking partner — one that never gets tired of exploring "what if" scenarios, summarizing research, and pointing out blind spots you might miss.

Used correctly, AI gives you a clearer picture of your choices and their potential outcomes. That means faster, better-informed decisions and a tighter feedback loop for improvement.

Why AI Works for Planning

Planning requires:

1. **Information gathering** – facts, figures, and relevant examples.
2. **Analysis** – connecting dots and identifying patterns.

3. **Scenario testing** – exploring the consequences of different moves.

4. **Iteration** – adapting based on results.

AI is strong in all four areas when given clear prompts and context. It's beneficial for small teams or solo operators who don't have an analyst, strategist, or researcher on staff.

Scenario Analysis: Stress-Testing Your Ideas

Scenario analysis is about mapping possible futures so you can prepare for them — not just hope for the best.

Example Use Case: You're deciding whether to launch a new product line. You want to see how it might play out under different market conditions.

Prompt: Create three scenarios for launching [product] in [market].

1. Best-case scenario: demand is high, supply chain is stable.

2. Moderate-case: demand meets projections, but supply chain delays occur.

3. Worst-case scenario: demand is low, and costs increase.

   For each scenario, outline likely revenue, risks, and mitigation strategies.

AI will produce narrative descriptions, risk factors, and sometimes even numerical ranges. You can refine these by feeding in your own past data or industry benchmarks.

SWOT Analysis with AI

SWOT (Strengths, Weaknesses, Opportunities, Threats) remains one of the most straightforward and useful planning tools. AI can speed up the brainstorming stage and push you to consider angles you might miss.

Prompt: Conduct a SWOT analysis for [business/product/idea] based on this description: [paste description]. Include at least 5 points for each category.

You can go deeper by chaining prompts:

- First, generate a broad SWOT.
- Then, ask AI to "prioritize the top 3 items in each category based on potential impact."
- Finally, have it "suggest strategic actions to maximize strengths and opportunities while minimizing weaknesses and threats."

Decision Matrices and Weighted Scoring

When you have multiple options, AI can help you build a simple decision matrix — a table that scores each option against the criteria you care about.

Example: Choosing between three marketing channels. Criteria might be cost, reach, speed, and alignment with your audience.

Prompt: Create a decision matrix comparing [Option A], [Option B], and [Option C] against these criteria: [list]. Weight cost at 40%, reach at 30%, speed at 20%, and alignment at 10%.

The result is a ranked recommendation — plus the reasoning behind the scores.

Tracking Progress with AI

Planning is only half the battle; tracking your plan's execution is where you keep momentum. AI can:

- Summarize weekly progress reports from raw updates.
- Flag risks when milestones are slipping.
- Suggest adjustments based on trends in the data.

Team members submit short weekly updates in a shared doc, and AI summarizes the data into what's on track, what's behind, and recommended following actions.

Prompt: From these weekly updates, create a summary of progress against goals. Highlight any risks or delays and suggest one adjustment per delayed task.

Iterating with AI Feedback Loops

Iteration is where AI truly excels, as it can rapidly reprocess updated data and provide new suggestions without starting from scratch.

Example loop:

1. You launch a marketing campaign.
2. AI helps you set KPIs (click-through rate, cost per lead, conversion rate).
3. After week one, you feed AI the results.
4. It compares against benchmarks and recommends tweaks.

Prompt: Based on this campaign data, identify what's working, what's underperforming, and recommend three specific changes for week two.

Using AI to Spot Blind Spots

AI can also play devil's advocate by poking holes in your plan.

Prompt: Critique this strategy for [goal]. Identify five potential flaws, oversights, or risks that I might not have considered.

This is especially valuable before big launches, partnerships, or investments. AI has no ego, so it will question things you might be emotionally attached to.

Case Study: AI Planning for a Local Service Business

A boutique gym wanted to expand into corporate wellness programs, but didn't know how to prioritize outreach.

Without AI: They were making calls to any company they could find, wasting time on low-potential leads.

With AI:

1. AI created a SWOT to identify the gym's strongest differentiators (personalized coaching, nutrition plans).
2. AI generated a list of high-value industries to target (tech companies, law firms) and ranked them by likely interest and budget.
3. AI ran scenario analysis for each target industry to estimate sales cycle length, potential deal size, and risks.
4. Monthly AI-generated progress reports kept them focused on the highest-return efforts.

Within three months, they had signed two corporate clients worth 5x their average customer value.

Limitations of AI in Decision Support

- AI doesn't have skin in the game — it can't replace your judgment.
- It may overconfidently present patterns that aren't statistically valid.
- Without accurate inputs, the outputs are just guesswork.

Always combine AI's analysis with your expertise and real-world validation.

Pro Tips for Better Planning Prompts

1. **Provide context** – including industry, goals, and constraints.
2. **Define success metrics** – what you're aiming for.
3. **Ask for structure** – tables, bullet points, or timelines- to make results easier to digest.
4. **Iterate** – refine outputs by feeding in your feedback or extra data.

Turning AI Planning into a Habit

Here's a weekly ritual you can adopt:

- **Monday:** Ask AI to summarize your current position and suggest priorities.
- **Midweek:** Feed in progress data; ask for quick adjustments.

- **Friday:** Run a short "lessons learned" review for the week.

This keeps your plans alive — not something you create once and forget.

Where AI Can't Replace You

- Setting the vision and overall direction.
- Balancing competing priorities.
- Making judgment calls in ambiguous situations.

AI is there to give you clarity and options — the choice remains yours.

Takeaways

- AI can significantly reduce the planning cycle while enhancing decision quality.
- Scenario analysis, SWOT analysis, and decision matrices provide structure to complex choices
- Tracking and iteration keep your plans relevant as conditions change.
- Use AI as a thinking partner, not an autopilot.

Next, we'll explore **RAG from Zero** — a chapter on connecting your AI tools to private, domain-specific data so you can answer questions with your knowledge base, not just what the AI was trained on.

PART III

Making AI Reliable

By now, you've seen AI create, research, and automate. But here's the truth: flashy demos are useless if the system isn't reliable. Part III is all about tightening the bolts, adding guardrails, and making sure your AI workflows don't just work once but work consistently. Here's the roadmap:

- **Chapter 11** introduces *RAG from Zero*—how to plug in your own data so AI isn't just guessing but answering with real context.
- **Chapter 12** takes you into *Tool and Function Calling*, where AI stops being just a chat partner and starts running tasks for you.
- **Chapter 13** is about *Evaluation and Guardrails*, where you test, measure, and adjust outputs to hit the quality you need.
- **Chapter 14** closes this section with *Cost and Latency Tuning*, because speed and budget matter just as much as clever answers.

This is where two parts of PROMPT show up big: **O (Optimize with AI)** and **T (Track & Tweak for Profit).**

Optimization here isn't about polishing sentences—it's about refining systems. AI models can be messy, and raw outputs can drift. Learning to optimize means setting up prompts, tools, and workflows so they produce consistent, high-quality results. Chapters 11 and 12 will show you how optimization goes beyond content into data pipelines and tool integrations.

But optimization without measurement is guesswork. That's where **T-Track & Tweak for Profit—**fits in. Chapter 13 makes this crystal clear: if you're not testing your AI outputs, you're leaving money and reputation on the table. Tracking lets you see if your chatbot answers well, if your generated posts perform, and if your automation saves time. Tuning is the step where minor adjustments unlock significant improvements—better margins, smoother delivery, fewer headaches.

By the time you finish Part III, you'll have systems you can trust. AI won't feel like a gamble anymore. It'll feel like infrastructure. And that's what separates dabblers from builders.

CHAPTER 11

RAG from Zero: Working with Your Own Data

Most people use AI models like ChatGPT, Claude, or Gemini as if they were search engines. They type in a question, get an answer, and assume the AI knows "everything." It doesn't. These models are trained on massive datasets, but they don't have your company's records, customer histories, or proprietary research baked in. That's where **RAG**, Retrieval-Augmented Generation, comes in.

RAG gives AI access to your data without retraining the model from scratch. You feed it the information it needs when it needs it. That's the difference between a general-purpose assistant and a specialist who knows your entire playbook.

What RAG Is (Without the Buzzwords)

Here's the simple breakdown:

- **Retrieval**: The AI searches through your own stored documents, notes, and datasets to find relevant chunks.
- **Augmentation**: It adds those chunks to the prompt so the AI has them in context.

- **Generation**: The AI writes its answer using both its general knowledge and your specific data.

It's like giving the AI a stack of carefully chosen cheat sheets right before you ask your question.

Why This Matters

Without RAG, AI is left to guess when you ask about your materials. If you ask, "What were our top-selling products in Q2?" a standard AI model will either invent numbers or say it can't access your data.

With RAG:

- You can load your Q2 sales report into a database.
- Ask the same question.
- The AI retrieves the relevant sales figures, then writes an accurate answer.

This is game-changing for businesses that need fast, accurate, and context-specific responses.

The Three Core Pieces of a RAG Setup

1. **Chunking** – Splitting your documents into small, searchable sections.
2. **Embedding** – Turning those chunks into numeric "fingerprints" that capture meaning.
3. **Retrieval** – Finding the most relevant chunks for your question and passing them to the AI.

Chunking: Breaking Data into Bite-Sized Pieces

You can't feed a 200-page manual into a single AI prompt — it's too big for the model's context window. So, you break it into "chunks" (often 200–1,000 words each).

The chunk size is a balancing act:

- **Too small** – The AI loses context and can't connect ideas.
- **Too large** – You waste space and might hit model limits.

Tip: Keep logical boundaries. Don't cut off mid-sentence or split a table in half.

Embedding: Turning Text into Searchable Vectors

Once you have chunks, you run them through an embedding model. This doesn't summarize them — it creates a mathematical representation of meaning.

Think of it like GPS coordinates for concepts. Instead of "123 Main Street," you get a set of numbers in a high-dimensional space that says, "This chunk is about warranty terms for product X."

Common embedding models:

- **OpenAI's text-embedding-3-large** – High accuracy, paid.
- **Sentence Transformers** – Popular open-source option.

Retrieval: Finding the Right Chunks Fast

When you ask a question, the system embeds your question into the same numeric space as your chunks. Finds the closest matches and passes them into the AI's prompt along with your question.

That's how it "remembers" your data — without having to store the whole manual in its head.

Storing Your Data Safely

For RAG to work, you need a storage layer. This is usually a vector database — a place built to store and search embeddings.

Popular options:

- **Pinecone** – Scalable, easy to use.
- **Weaviate** – Open-source with strong community support.
- **FAISS** – Facebook's open-source library for local storage.

If privacy is critical, you can run your vector DB entirely on your server, so no third party ever touches your data.

RAG in Practice: A Simple Workflow

Let's say you run a law firm and want AI to answer client intake questions based on your internal handbook.

1. **Collect Documents** – PDF handbook, internal training notes, and FAQ sheets.
2. **Chunk Documents** – Split into ~500-word sections with clear headings.
3. **Create Embeddings** – Use an embedding model to turn chunks into vectors.

4. **Store in Vector DB** – Save all embeddings in Pinecone or a local FAISS instance.

5. **Ask a Question** – "What is our standard retainer fee for new corporate clients?"

6. **Retrieve Relevant Chunks** – The system pulls the chunk with the fee details.

7. **Generate Answer** – AI writes the reply using both handbook content and its language skills.

Handling Updates

Businesses change. If your pricing, processes, or policies change, your RAG system must reflect those changes.

- **Automate ingestion**: Have your RAG pipeline check a folder for new/updated files and re-embed them automatically.

- **Version control**: Keep a log of when each document was last updated.

- **Archive old data**: Remove outdated chunks to prevent them from mixing with current ones.

Avoiding Common Mistakes

1. **Overstuffing context** – Just because you *can* pass 20 chunks doesn't mean you should. The more you load, the less focus the AI has on each piece.

2. **Mixing unrelated data** – If your knowledge base has HR policies following engineering documentation, retrieval relevance can suffer. Keep separate indexes for different domains.

3. **Skipping quality checks** – Always test your RAG system with tricky edge cases to see if it pulls the right chunks.

Example Prompts with RAG

When using RAG, your prompts get simpler because the relevant data is already in context. Instead of: Summarize our 2023 refund policy from the attached document.

You ask: What's our current refund policy? The retrieval step handles finding the correct section for you.

Security and Privacy Considerations

When your AI system has access to private data, you need to think about:

- **Data encryption** (at rest and in transit).
- **Access controls** ensure that only approved individuals can query specific indexes.
- **Audit logs** to track who searched for what and when.

If your data is extremely sensitive, stick with on-premise or private cloud solutions — don't feed it to public APIs without clear contracts.

Case Study: RAG for a Small Manufacturing Company

A 25-person manufacturer had hundreds of spec sheets, repair guides, and process documents scattered in PDFs. Employees wasted hours searching for answers to client questions.

Before RAG:

- Repeated calls to engineering for basic info.

- Slow email replies to customers.

After RAG Implementation:

- Documents chunked, embedded, and stored in Pinecone.
- An AI assistant built to retrieve specs instantly.
- Average customer email reply time dropped from 2 days to 30 minutes.

Beyond Text: RAG for Other Data Types

While most RAG setups work with text, you can also retrieve:

- **Images** – by embedding visual features.
- **Audio** – after transcription.
- **Structured data** – like CSVs or databases.

This means your "knowledge base" could include product photos, call recordings, and even spreadsheets.

How to Start Small

You don't need a whole engineering team to try RAG.

1. Pick **one document set** — like your top 10 internal guides.
2. Use a low-code tool like **LangChain** + Pinecone or **LlamaIndex** to set up chunking and retrieval.
3. Test with a few high-value queries.

Once it works, expand your index gradually.

Takeaways

- RAG lets you feed AI your knowledge without retraining.
- The key steps are **chunking**, **embedding**, and **retrieval**.
- Store data securely in a vector DB, and update it regularly.
- Start small, test for accuracy, then expand.

In the next chapter, we'll talk about **Tool and Function Calling** — the next step after retrieval, where AI doesn't just find information but acts in your other systems.

CHAPTER 12

Tool and Function Calling

An intelligent assistant that can only talk is helpful. A smart assistant that can act is powerful. This is where Tool and Function Calling comes in — the bridge between AI's natural language abilities and the real-world tools you use every day.

Instead of stopping at "Here's how you could do it," a function-enabled AI can go further: run the query, pull the data, generate the chart, and send the email. It's the shift from advice to execution.

What Tool and Function Calling Means

The term "function calling" can sound overly technical, but the concept is simple:

1. You give AI a goal in plain language.
2. It determines which function (or tool) can accomplish that.
3. It sends structured instructions to that function.
4. The function returns results.
5. The AI continues the conversation or chains the results into the next step.

Think of it like asking a human assistant to "book a flight," and instead of writing down a list of travel websites for you to check, they go and book the flight based on your preferences.

Why This Is a Big Deal

Without function calling, you must be the middleman — copy-pasting AI's recommendations into your apps, running the searches, importing the results back.

With function calling:

- AI can directly interact with your CRM, databases, or analytics platform.
- You can automate multi-step workflows without manually gluing each step together.
- The same conversation can contain both decision-making and action-taking.

Everyday Use Cases for Tool/Function Calling

- **Database queries** – "Show me sales for Q2 by region."
- **API integrations** – pulling live data from weather, stock, or shipping APIs.
- **Document creation** – auto-generating and storing PDFs, Word docs, or slides.
- **Scheduling** – booking calendar events based on context from emails.
- **Report automation** – building recurring reports with fresh data.

- **Customer service** – pulling up order details while chatting with a customer.

The Building Blocks

To connect AI to tools, you need three main parts:

1. **Functions or APIs** – the actual capabilities you want to trigger.
2. **Schema** – the "instructions manual" that tells AI what arguments the function takes.
3. **Permissions** – guardrails that keep the AI from doing something you didn't intend.

Example: Auto-Generating Reports

Let's walk through a realistic example: a weekly sales report that usually takes you two hours to compile.

Goal: Get an AI assistant to pull sales data from your database, format it into a report, and send it to your team.

Define and Connect the AI to These Functions

Your AI system now knows that when you say:

"Create the weekly sales report for August 1–7 and send it to the sales team." …it needs to call the three functions in order. In minutes, the job is done without you touching a spreadsheet or email client.

Security and Access Control

A tool-enabled AI can be dangerous if not properly scoped. You don't want it emailing clients or deleting records without explicit approval.

Best practices:

- **Read-only mode** for sensitive databases unless write access is required.
- **Approval prompts** – AI asks for confirmation before performing irreversible actions.
- **Logging** – Every function call is recorded for audit purposes.

How It Fits into Everyday Workflows

Once you set up tool calling, you can start blending research, planning, and execution in a single thread.

Example:

- **You:** "Summarize this month's support tickets and create a chart of the top 5 issue types."
- **AI:** Pulls data via the support desk API, processes it, generates the chart, and embeds it in a PDF.
- **You:** "Send this to the product team and add it to the sprint planning doc."
- **AI:** Emails, PDFs, and updates your project management tool.

Low-Code and No-Code Options

You don't need to write all this from scratch. Platforms like:

- **Zapier AI Actions** – Let AI run Zaps from chat.
- **Make.com + OpenAI** – Build custom workflows triggered by AI prompts.

- **Retool / n8n** – For more complex in-house dashboards.

These handle the plumbing so you can focus on defining what you want done.

Beyond APIs: Native Tool Integrations

Some AI platforms now have built-in connectors to apps like Google Sheets, Slack, and Notion. That means you can skip the custom API setup and authorize the connection.

Example: "Add these 10 leads to my CRM" → AI directly updates Salesforce without you touching the interface.

Best Practices for Designing Tool-Enabled Prompts

1. **Be explicit about the action** – "Generate," "Send," "Save," "Update."
2. **Define parameters clearly** – Dates, names, formats.
3. **State the output format** – PDF, CSV, chart, etc.
4. **Include constraints** – "No emails to customers until I confirm."

Case Study: AI in Finance Operations

A mid-sized e-commerce brand utilized an AI tool to automate its end-of-month financial summaries.

Before:

- Manually exporting sales from Shopify.
- Merging with ad spend reports.
- Formatting into Google Slides for stakeholders.

After:

- AI connected to Shopify API + Google Ads API.
- Pulled and reconciled sales/ad spend in one pass.
- Generated the slide deck with updated graphs.
- Emailed the deck to the leadership team automatically.

Time saved: 12–15 hours per month.

Combining RAG and Tool Calling

The last chapter covered RAG for private data retrieval. Pairing it with tool calling allows AI not only to find the right internal policy but also to apply it.

Example: "Send all clients with overdue invoices a reminder based on our collections policy."

- RAG retrieves the collections policy.
- The tool identifies overdue accounts in your accounting system.
- The tool call sends reminders using approved language.

Limitations to Watch Out For

- **Garbage in, garbage out** – If APIs return messy or outdated data, AI will act on it without knowing better.
- **Latency** – Some APIs are slow, which can make AI responses lag.
- **Cost creep** – Every API call and AI action may have a per-use fee.

Getting Started in a Weekend

1. Pick one repetitive task (like generating a weekly report).
2. List the tools involved and check if they have APIs.
3. Set up a simple function call between AI and one API.
4. Test with dummy data until you trust the flow.
5. Gradually add more tools/functions into the chain.

Function calling turns AI from an advisor into an operator. It bridges conversation and execution, letting you handle research, decision-making, and action in one loop. In the next chapter, we'll cover **Evaluation and Guardrails** — how to keep your AI reliable, accurate, and safe even as you automate more of your work.

CHAPTER 13

Evaluation and Guardrails

The more you rely on AI, the more you must face a simple truth: It's not always right.

AI can produce polished, confident-sounding answers that are entirely wrong. Sometimes it misinterprets your question. Sometimes it invents facts (hallucination). And sometimes it reflects bias or patterns you didn't intend.

If you're building AI into your workflows — especially in business-critical tasks — you can't just trust the first thing it spits out. You need a system to evaluate outputs, detect problems, and put guardrails in place so errors don't cause real-world damage.

O – Optimize with AI

Optimization doesn't stop at prompts. The O in PROMPT reappears here—Optimize with AI—by evaluating responses and tightening guardrails. When you test and refine outputs, you move from sloppy drafts to dependable systems.

T – Track & Tweak for Profit

Evaluation is just another angle of the T step—Track & Tweak for Profit. You measure outputs, spot flaws, and adjust until the system is tight. The same mindset that improves AI prompts also improves your bottom line.

Why Evaluation Matters

AI is probabilistic, not deterministic. That means it's generating the most likely next word or action based on patterns — not verifying truth against a master database.

If you don't evaluate:

- **Insufficient data slips in** and gets repeated.
- **Biases** can skew recommendations.
- **Safety risks** often go unnoticed until they affect customers or systems.

Think of it like having an intern who works incredibly fast but sometimes makes things up — you still must check their work before sending it to a client.

The Three Layers of Evaluation

When working with AI in real operations, you should think about three checkpoints:

1. **Spot-Checking Outputs** – Quick sanity checks after each task.
2. **Bias and Risk Detection** – Identifying patterns that could cause harm or mislead.
3. **Automated Guardrails** – Systems that prevent dangerous or costly outputs from ever being used.

Spot-Checking Outputs

Spot-checking doesn't mean reading every word in every AI-generated document — it means checking the correc*t* parts before approving.

What to look for:

- **Obvious factual errors** – Names, dates, numbers.
- **Logical inconsistencies** – A plan that contradicts itself.
- **Formatting issues** – Missing sections, broken tables.
- **Language tone** – Does it match your brand or purpose?

Pro tip: Create a short checklist for each output type. For example, if you're reviewing AI-generated blog posts, your checklist might be:

1. Fact-check all statistics.
2. Verify quotes or sources.
3. Confirm internal links are correct.

Bias and Risk Detection

AI models learn from real-world data, which means they inherit the biases inherent in that data. Sometimes subtle, sometimes blatant.

Bias types to watch for:

- **Demographic bias** – Over-representing one group in examples or recommendations.
- **Selection bias** – Favoring specific data sources without justification.

- **Confirmation bias** – Overweighting info that supports the initial prompt.

Risk areas:

- **Legal** – Making claims you can't substantiate.
- **Ethical** – Suggesting strategies that exploit customers or break trust.
- **Operational** – Giving instructions that, if followed literally, could cause harm or loss.

Prompt: Review the following output for potential demographic, cultural, or logical bias. List any issues found and suggest neutral alternatives.

Automated Guardrails

If you're running AI at scale, you can't rely solely on human review — you need automated checks.

Examples:

- **Keyword filters** – Block outputs containing banned terms.
- **Regex checks** – Validate formats (e.g., phone numbers, dates).
- **External verification APIs** – Check generated facts against known databases.
- **Safe action limits** – If a tool call tries to delete more than 50 records, require manual confirmation.

Guardrails don't replace human oversight — they stop obvious problems before they reach you.

Knowing When to Reject AI Output

Sometimes "good enough" is fine. Sometimes you must hit delete and start over.

Reject if:

- The core facts are wrong.
- The structure doesn't match your needs.
- It's faster to re-do than to fix.
- There's a risk of reputational or legal harm.

And if you do reject it, don't just say "try again" — tell the AI what failed so the next attempt is better.

Iterating for Quality

A strong evaluation loop looks like this:

1. Generate the output.
2. Review against your checklist.
3. Flag issues and explain why they're issues.
4. Regenerate or manually fix.
5. Store the "approved" example for future training/reference.

This is how you teach AI to consistently hit your target style and accuracy — even if you're not fine-tuning the model.

Evaluating with Metrics

Beyond gut feeling, you can apply measurable metrics:

- **Accuracy rate** – % of outputs that pass without significant changes.
- **Time to approve** – How long does it take to go from an AI draft to a final version?
- **Error severity** – Track not just the number of errors, but how costly they'd be if unnoticed.

Case Study: Guardrails in Customer Support AI

A SaaS company used AI to draft customer support replies. At first, it was fast — but they quickly realized some replies included outdated policy details.

Fix:

- Added a RAG layer to ensure AI always references the latest policy documents.
- Added a guardrail that flagged any mention of refund periods for human review.
- Trained support leads conduct spot-checks on 10% of replies daily.

Result: Accuracy rate jumped from 82% to 97%, and customers stopped receiving conflicting answers.

Practical Prompts for Evaluation

- **Fact-checking:**

Review this draft for factual accuracy. Highlight any statements that require a source or verification.

- **Risk scanning:**

Scan this text for potential legal, ethical, or operational risks. Suggest safer wording if needed.

- **Bias check:**

Analyze this response for cultural or demographic bias. Recommend more inclusive alternatives.

- **Quality scoring:**

Score this output from 1–10 for clarity, accuracy, and usefulness. Explain your reasoning.

Guardrails for Different Output Types

Content Creation:

- Require source citations for claims.
- Block publishing if plagiarism is detected.

Code Generation:

- Run automated security linting before deployment.
- Block code that modifies specific protected files.

Data Analysis:

- Cross-check with original datasets.

- Flag statistical outputs with confidence intervals.

Dealing with "Hallucinations"

Hallucinations occur when AI confidently fabricates something. Common triggers:

- Asking for specific numbers without providing data.
- Asking about niche topics not in the training set.
- Combining multiple vague instructions into one answer.

How to reduce them:

- Use RAG to feed real data into the prompt.
- Ask for uncertainty levels ("If unsure, say you don't know").
- Force step-by-step reasoning instead of final answers only.

When AI Should Stop and Ask

Sometimes, the safest guardrail is to make AI *ask* before guessing.
Example:

If the customer order ID is not found in the database, ask me how to proceed instead of creating an answer.

This keeps you in the loop for high-risk actions.

From Limitations to Reliability

If Chapter 8 was about knowing AI's limits, this chapter is about operationalizing that knowledge.

The goal isn't to make AI perfect — that's impossible. The goal is to make its mistakes predictable, catchable, and fixable before they cause harm.

Takeaways

- Always layer human review + automated checks.
- Use targeted prompts for bias, risk, and factual accuracy.
- Set guardrails that block dangerous or costly mistakes.
- Know when to reject output entirely.
- Track quality over time to measure improvement.

Next up, we'll dig into **Cost and Latency Tuning** — how to make AI faster and cheaper without cutting corners on quality.

CHAPTER 14

Cost and Latency Tuning

You can have the most innovative AI system in the world, but if it costs more than it earns — or takes too long to respond — it's not sustainable. AI needs to run like a business asset, not a science experiment. That means two things:

1. Keep expenses predictable and reasonable.
2. Keep the system fast enough that users don't abandon it out of frustration.

This is where cost and latency tuning come in.

Why It Matters

- **High costs** eat into profits, especially if you're offering AI-powered services to clients on fixed fees.
- **High latency** (slow response times) kills adoption — users expect AI to feel instant, not like waiting for dial-up in 1998.
- A well-tuned system enables scaling without incurring unnecessary expenses or losing customers.

The trick is finding that sweet spot between speed, quality, and cost.

Know Where the Money Goes

Before you can reduce costs, you must understand them. AI-related expenses usually break down into:

- **API calls** – Paid per request, per token, or both.
- **Data storage** – Vector databases, logs, backups.
- **Third-party services** – Zapier, Make.com, hosting, analytics tools.
- **Development and maintenance** – Not just building, but keeping things running.

If you don't track these separately, you can't tell which lever to pull.

Pro tip: Always run a cost-per-output analysis. If it costs $1 to generate a social media post and you're selling them for $0.75, you're bleeding money.

Right-Size Your Models

Most people use the biggest, most expensive model for *everything*. That's like using a Ferrari to run grocery errands.

- Use smaller models for simple tasks like keyword extraction or sentiment analysis.
- Reserve larger models for complex reasoning or creative work.
- Consider open-source models (like LLaMA or Mistral) for high-volume, low-sensitivity tasks where privacy is key.

Example:

Customer support bot → Use a small, fast model for FAQs. If the query is complex, escalate to a bigger model.

Control Token Usage

Every token you send to and from the AI costs money and time. Tokens are just chunks of text, but they add up fast.

Ways to cut token usage:

- **Trim prompts** – Remove fluff from system messages.
- **Summarize history** – Instead of passing the whole conversation, keep a rolling summary.
- **Set max tokens** – Don't let outputs balloon unnecessarily.

Case in point:

A marketing team cut API costs by 42% just by shortening prompt instructions and reducing output length from 1,200 words to 800 for blog drafts.

Cache Repeatable Results

If you keep asking AI the same thing, store the answer and reuse it.

- Cache "static" outputs — product descriptions, bios, and FAQ answers.
- Cache intermediate processing — if you already cleaned a dataset yesterday, don't re-clean it today.

This is especially valuable when combined with **RAG** (Chapter 11), so AI can fetch cached content instead of regenerating it.

Tune for Latency Without Killing Quality

Latency is simply the time it takes to receive a response. Too slow, and people get impatient. Too fast, and you might be sacrificing depth.

Factors that affect latency:

- **Model size** – Bigger models think more slowly.
- **Prompt length** – More text in = more time to process.
- **External calls** – Waiting for APIs, database queries, or file uploads.

Ways to reduce latency:

- Use streaming output so users see the answer as it's being generated.
- Pre-fetch data you know you'll need before the user asks.
- Split big tasks into smaller ones and run them in parallel.

Batch Operations

If you have multiple similar tasks, process them in batches.

Example: Instead of generating 50 ad headlines one at a time, send them in one prompt and parse the results.

- Saves on tokens.
- Cuts down on connection overhead.

Choose the Right Context Window

Large context windows allow the AI to "remember" more, but they come at a higher cost and slow things down.

- For chatbots, use a short-term memory and a summary of key points.
- For document analysis, feed only the relevant chunks (see RAG).

Optimize Retrieval and Preprocessing

If you're running RAG or tool integrations, preprocessing steps can eat up time.

- Store data in ready-to-use formats (e.g., JSON for structured data).
- Index documents once instead of re-indexing every time.
- Keep vector search queries tight — don't pull 50 chunks when five will do.

Monitor in Real Time

You can't tune what you don't measure.

- Track **cost per request**, **average latency**, and **error rates** daily or weekly.
- Use dashboards from providers like OpenAI, Anthropic, or your hosting platform.
- Watch for cost spikes — they usually mean something's looping or stuck.

Build Fallback Plans

Even with perfect tuning, APIs go down or slow to a crawl.

- Have a **backup model** to handle overflow.
- Serve cached answers during downtime.
- For critical systems, run two providers in parallel and take the fastest result.

Example: Cost and Latency Tuning in a Real Business

A content marketing agency was producing hundreds of AI-assisted blog posts per month.

Before tuning:

- Every post was processed through GPT-4, incurring $1.40 in API fees each.
- Average turnaround per post was 2–3 minutes.

After tuning:

- Simple research tasks moved to a smaller model at $0.15 per post.
- Drafting split between GPT-3.5 for structure and GPT-4 only for polishing.
- Prompt instructions shortened by 30%.
- Posts now take 45 seconds on average, with a 60% reduction in cost.

Result: The agency scaled output by 3x without increasing its budget.

Cost and Latency Trade-offs

Sometimes you can't have both the cheapest and the fastest option.

- **If quality is king,** accept slower responses for critical outputs.
- **If speed wins:** Use smaller, cheaper models even if the writing isn't as refined — then polish later.

Pro Tips for Keeping Things Balanced

- **Hybrid approach**: Route tasks dynamically based on complexity.
- **Token budgeting**: Decide in advance how many tokens each task type gets.
- **Model warmup**: Keep your most-used model active so the first request isn't delayed.
- **Async workflows**: For background tasks, let them run slower if it saves cost — users don't need them instantly.

Tool Stack for Cost/Latency Management

- **LangSmith or PromptLayer** – Track prompt cost and performance.
- **Vercel Edge Functions** – Deploy close to users for faster response times.
- **Redis / Memcached** – Cache frequent results.
- **Pinecone / Weaviate** – Vector storage for RAG with fast retrieval.

The Mindset Shift

Cost and latency tuning isn't about squeezing AI until it's lifeless. It's about **right-sizing** the process to maximize business value per dollar.

If you ignore it, AI becomes an expensive, slow novelty. If you master it, AI becomes a lean, responsive workhorse you can rely on at scale.

Next, we'll go into **Monetization Paths** — turning all these tuned, efficient AI systems into real revenue streams without falling into the trap of over-promising and under-delivering.

PART IV

Monetization Paths

So far, you've learned how AI works, how to build workflows, and how to make those workflows reliable. Now comes the part most readers are waiting for: turning all of that into money. Part IV is where the outputs start paying rent.

This section is structured around real monetization channels—ways people are already using AI to generate revenue, often with very little startup capital:

- **Chapter 15** shows how to package AI-driven services and sell them directly—think client projects, freelancing, and consulting.
- **Chapter 16** moves into *Digital Products with AI*, where you create assets once and sell them again and again.
- **Chapter 17** dives into *Niche Media and Content Brands*, where publishing with consistency and strategy builds long-term equity.
- **Chapter 18** explores *Agency-Lite Automations*, where you sell the system itself instead of the output, giving businesses the back-end leverage they don't know how to build.

- **Chapter 19** pulls it all together with pricing strategies and simple unit economics, so you don't just sell but profit.

This entire section is the **M in PROMPT—Monetize via Platforms.** Here's the key: the platforms already exist. Etsy, Gumroad, Amazon KDP, YouTube, TikTok, Upwork, Fiverr—they're built, they're trusted, and they already have traffic. You don't need to reinvent distribution. You need to plug your optimized AI outputs into places where money already flows.

Part IV will show you the many shapes that can take:

- Service platforms where AI helps you deliver faster than the competition.
- Product platforms where you create once and sell forever.
- Media platforms where publishing and promoting compounds into audience growth.
- Automation platforms where you become the middle layer between businesses and the AI tools they can't figure out.

The through-line is simple: AI is leveraged, but platforms are the marketplace. Put them together, and you get monetization that's faster, cheaper, and more scalable than traditional methods.

By the end of Part IV, you won't just know how to make something with AI—you'll know exactly where to put it so it makes money.

CHAPTER 15

Service Offers with AI

If you've been following along, you now have a toolkit that can research, write, summarize, plan, and automate — faster than you ever could alone. That's powerful. But tools alone don't make money. Offers do.

An offer is how you package your skills and deliver them in a way people will pay for. The AI is just the engine under the hood. The business is in knowing what problem you solve, who it's for, and how you deliver it.

M – Monetize via Platforms

Here's the M in PROMPT: Monetize via Platforms. Service work is the fastest way to earn, and AI makes it easier. Offer client-ready deliverables on Fiverr, Upwork, or even LinkedIn—fast, polished, and priced right.

Why AI is a Service Multiplier

AI isn't a service by itself — it's a service multiplier. You can take something people already pay for (copywriting, data analysis, customer service, marketing strategy) and deliver it:

- Faster
- At higher volume

- For a competitive price
- With more personalization

That means as a freelancer, consultant, or agency owner, you can either:

1. Offer the same service but with better margins, or
2. Offer a more premium service at the exact cost because your output is richer.

Pick Your Service Lane

If you try to sell "AI services" as a generic product, you'll disappear into the noise. Instead, sell a result in a specific domain.

Examples:

- Social media content calendars for small businesses.
- Product description writing for e-commerce stores.
- Data cleaning and dashboard building for real estate agencies.
- Proposal writing for B2B contractors.

Pick a lane that:

- You understand well enough to talk to clients in their language.
- Has demand you can validate (people already buying).
- Can benefit from AI's speed and pattern recognition.

Decide Your Delivery Model

There are three main models you can run:

1. Freelancing

You sell your time or a fixed package directly to clients. Platforms like Upwork, Fiverr, and Contra can help you get started quickly.

- **Pros:** Low overhead, easy to start.
- **Cons:** Income depends on constant client work; competitive pricing pressure.

2. Consulting

You sell your expertise and strategic thinking — the AI is a behind-the-scenes accelerant.

- **Pros:** Higher fees, less execution work.
- **Cons:** Requires credibility and strong communication skills.

3. Agency Work

You build a small team (which could be you and AI at first) and deliver services at scale.

- **Pros:** More capacity, recurring revenue potential.
- **Cons:** More moving parts; need processes.

Define Your AI-Boosted Process

Your value isn't just in using AI — it's in how you use it to make the client's life easier.

Example for a content marketing service:

1. Client fills out a short form about their business.
2. AI creates a content calendar for 30 days.
3. AI drafts all 30 posts with captions and hashtags.
4. You review, edit, and deliver content according to a posting schedule.

That's a complete, repeatable workflow — not just "I'll write posts for you."

Price with Confidence

You don't have to price low just because AI makes the work faster. Clients pay for outcomes, not hours.

Pricing options:

- **Flat project fee** – Great for repeatable deliverables (e.g., $300 for a 30-day content package).
- **Retainer** – Ongoing work at a set monthly fee.
- **Day rate** – Intensive 1–2 day "done-for-you" sprints.

Pro tip: Anchor your price to the *value* of the outcome. If your AI-driven ad copy can lift conversions by 20%, that's worth far more than the time it took to generate it.

Make the Offer Easy to Say Yes To

A firm offer removes friction for the buyer.

- Clear deliverables ("You get X posts, Y graphics, Z hashtags").

- Timeline ("Delivered in 5 days").
- Low-risk first step ("Start with a 1-week trial").

You can even frame the AI part as an advantage:

"I combine expert strategy with cutting-edge AI tools to deliver in days what normally takes weeks — without sacrificing quality."

Examples of AI-Powered Service Offers

Copywriting & Content

- Blog posts, SEO articles, newsletters.
- Product descriptions for e-commerce stores.
- Email sequences for sales funnels.

AI advantage: You can produce 3–5 polished drafts in the time it takes a traditional writer to make one.

Marketing & Advertising

- Ad copy variations for A/B testing.
- Social media post batches.
- Campaign ideation based on trends and audience insights.

AI advantage: Instantly test more variations and adapt campaigns faster.

Research & Analysis

- Competitor intelligence summaries.
- Industry trend reports.

- Customer feedback analysis.

AI advantage: Rapid synthesis of large datasets into clear, actionable reports.

Data and Ops

- CRM cleanup and deduplication.
- Weekly reporting dashboards.
- Automated lead scoring.

AI advantage: Turn hours of manual sorting into minutes of automated analysis.

Build Your First Case Study Fast

Your first few clients might not care about AI — they care about results. To get traction:

- Offer an introductory rate for your first project.
- Deliver the results and document them.
- Turn that into a short case study with before-and-after metrics.

Before: Client posting irregularly, low engagement. **After:** 30-day AI-assisted calendar → 3x engagement, two new leads.

Market Yourself Without Burning Out

You don't have to be on every platform. Choose one outbound channel and one inbound channel.

- **Outbound:** Cold email, LinkedIn DMs, platform proposals.
- **Inbound:** Content marketing, SEO blog, lead magnet.

Pro tip: Use AI to draft your pitches and proposals, but customize each one enough that it doesn't feel generic.

Use AI for Client Management Too

AI isn't just for deliverables — it can save time on client relationships:

- Drafting meeting recaps.
- Turning feedback into clear revision lists.
- Automatically creating upsell proposals after a project.

This keeps your delivery smooth and gives you more bandwidth for high-value work.

Turn Your Service into a Productized Offer

Once you've done a few projects, look for patterns:

- Which parts are always the same?
- Which can be fully automated?
- Which steps always get client praise?

Turn that into a productized offer with a name, price, and standard process. This is how you move from "freelancer" to "business owner." Instead of "I write social posts," it's "30-Day Authority Builder — 30 custom posts, captions, and graphics delivered in 5 days for $349."

Scale Without Losing Quality

As demand grows, you have options:

- **Hire human help** for the parts AI can't handle well (strategy, brand voice polishing).
- **Automate more** with RAG, tool calling, and integrations.
- **Niche down further** to charge more for specialized expertise.

Pitfalls to Avoid

- **Selling AI instead of selling results.** People don't buy "AI content"; they buy "more sales," "more traffic," or "less work."
- **Overpromising on quality.** AI is a tool — you still need human review.
- **Ignoring client education.** Some clients may distrust AI; show them examples to help them understand its value.

Quick Start Plan: Your First AI Service Offer in a Week

Day 1: Pick your service lane.

Day 2: Define your process and deliverables.

Day 3: Create a one-page offer sheet with price and timeline.

Day 4: Build one example project as a portfolio piece.

Day 5: Reach out to 10 potential clients.

Day 6: Follow up and tweak your pitch based on responses.

Day 7: Land your first paid project.

AI makes you faster. A well-crafted offer makes you profitable. Combine the two, and you're not just selling services — you're selling speed, scale, and certainty in a market that's hungry for all three.

The next chapter will cover **Digital Products with AI** — so you can take your expertise and package it into something you sell over and over without doing the work each time.

CHAPTER 16

Digital Products with AI

When you offer a service, your income is tied to your time. When you create a digital product, your time becomes decoupled from your income. You make it once, and it continues to earn.

That's the power of digital products — and AI makes creating them faster, cheaper, and easier than ever.

P – Position Your Niche

This is where the first step of the PROMPT Goldmine System™—Position Your Niche—becomes real. Most creators go too broad, and they end up invisible. Use AI tools to test different micro-niches until you find one with demand but low competition. Think sniper rifle, not shotgun.

M – Monetize via Platforms

Once your niche is positioned, shift into M—Monetize via Platforms. Digital downloads on Etsy, templates on Gumroad, or AI-assisted books on Amazon KDP. Each is a low-barrier entry to cash flow.

Why Digital Products Work So Well with AI

Digital products are infinitely replicable. Once made, they cost nothing to deliver.

AI accelerates the creation and iteration process:

- You can brainstorm and validate ideas in hours instead of weeks.
- You can create polished, ready-to-sell assets without hiring a team.
- You can update your product quickly to keep it fresh. .

The result? A scalable, low-overhead business model that can stack on top of your service offers or stand alone as its own income stream.

The Main Types of AI-Boosted Digital Products

We'll focus on three high-profit categories you can start with today:

1. **Templates** – Pre-made assets people can customize.
2. **Courses** – Structured learning experiences.
3. **Printables** – Downloadable designs, planners, or checklists.

Templates: The Shortcut People Pay For

Templates are about time savings. People buy them to skip the blank-page problem.

Examples:

- Social media post templates for Instagram or LinkedIn.

- Email marketing sequences for coaches.
- Proposal templates for freelancers.
- Spreadsheet calculators for budgeting or project management.

How AI helps:

- Generate multiple style variations in minutes.
- Pre-fill examples so users see exactly how it works.
- Write detailed usage instructions and quick-start guides.

Workflow:

Pick a niche and product type (e.g., "Instagram Story templates for nutrition coaches")—prompt AI to create 20 post outlines, captions, and call-to-action ideas. Use Canva or Figma to design graphics. Bundle into a ZIP file with an instruction PDF.

Pro tip: Give your templates a theme or purpose ("30-Day Client-Attracting Stories") instead of selling a generic pack.

Courses: Teach What You Know

Online courses are booming because people are willing to pay to acquire skills they believe will yield tangible results.

Examples:

- "AI for Small Business Owners"
- "ChatGPT for Real Estate Agents"
- "Etsy Success with AI-Generated Designs"

How AI helps:

- Outline your course structure based on your expertise and competitor research.
- Script lessons in your voice.
- Generate quizzes, worksheets, and case studies to increase engagement.

Workflow:

Define your transformation promise ("You'll go from zero to publishing your first Etsy listing in 7 days").

Break it into modules and lessons.

Use AI to script each lesson, then record using Loom, ScreenFlow, or your phone.

Upload to a course platform like Teachable, Thinkific, or Kajabi.

Add AI-generated workbook PDFs for added value.

Pro tip: Short courses (1–2 hours total) sell well at $49–$99, and are easier to create and launch than full-blown programs.

Printables: Instant Gratification Products

Printables are low-cost, high-volume products people can download and use immediately. They're especially popular on Etsy, Creative Market, and niche Shopify stores.

Examples:

- Wedding planners.

- Daily, weekly, or monthly trackers.
- Goal-setting journals.
- Meal prep calendars.

How AI helps:

- Generate layouts and copy for planners and checklists.
- Suggest themed variations for seasonal launches.
- Write compelling product descriptions optimized for Etsy search.

Workflow:

Pick a functional or decorative printable idea. Have AI generate copy for headings, instructions, and prompts. Design in Canva or Affinity Publisher. Export as PDF—list on a marketplace with optimized keywords.

Pro tip: Bundle related printables into kits — they sell for more and feel like a better deal.

Finding a Profitable Digital Product Idea

Don't start by asking "What can I make?" Start with "What do people already pay for?"

Idea validation steps:

Search Etsy, Gumroad, and Creative Market for your category.

Sort by "Bestselling" or "Top Rated" to see proven products.

Read reviews to spot gaps or improvement opportunities.

Use AI to brainstorm differentiators.

Prompt: Based on these top-selling Etsy listings for wedding planners, suggest 10 unique angles or features I could add to make my product stand out.

Packaging Your Product for Perceived Value

How you present the product matters almost as much as the product itself.

- Use mockups to show the product "in action" (Canva has free ones).
- Include an instruction or quick-start guide so buyers feel confident.
- Bundle bonus items that are easy for you to make but valuable to them.

Pricing and Positioning

Digital products can sell anywhere from $5 to $500, depending on complexity and perceived value.

- Templates: $10–$49 for single packs, $99+ for bundles.
- Short courses: $49–$99, higher if in-demand skill.
- Printables: $5–$25 for singles, $15–$50 for bundles.

You can also use a low-cost product as a lead magnet — get someone into your world with a $9 printable, then upsell them to a $99 course.

AI Tools to Streamline Creation

- **ChatGPT / Claude / Gemini** – Scriptwriting, outlines, brainstorming.
- **Canva / Figma** – Design templates and printables.
- **Midjourney / DALL·E** – Custom illustrations and visuals.
- **Descript / ScreenFlow** – Video lesson recording and editing.

Selling Your Digital Products

Marketplaces:

- Etsy – Great for printables and templates.
- Creative Market – Design-heavy products.
- Udemy – Lower-priced, high-volume courses.
- Gumroad – Flexible for all types.

Your site:

- More control and higher margins.
- Use Shopify, WooCommerce, or Podia.

Pro tip: Even if you sell mainly on marketplaces, capture email addresses so you can sell future products directly.

Marketing Without a Huge Ad Budget

- Use Pinterest for visual products — pins can drive traffic for years.

- Share short demo videos on TikTok and Instagram.
- Offer free samples in exchange for joining your email list.

AI can generate marketing assets in batches, allowing you to post consistently without spending hours each week.

Keeping Your Product Fresh

Unlike a book, digital products can be updated anytime.

- Refresh templates with new designs.
- Add bonus lessons to courses.
- Create seasonal variations of printables.

Updates give you a reason to email past customers — and sell them the new version.

Stacking Digital Products into an Ecosystem

One product is good. A **product ladder** is better.

Example:

- Entry: $9 "Mini Planner" printable.
- Mid-tier: $49 "Business Planning Template Kit."
- High-tier: $199 "6-Week Strategic Planning Course."

Each product leads to the next, increasing lifetime value without the need to constantly chase new customers.

Pitfalls to Avoid

- **Overbuilding before selling.** Validate with a minimum viable version first.

- **Ignoring design.** Even if the content is solid, poor visuals will kill sales.
- **Underpricing premium work.** Just because AI speeds you up doesn't mean your product is worth less.

Quick Start Plan: Launch Your First AI Digital Product in 14 Days

Day 1–2: Research bestsellers and validate your idea.

Day 3–5: Outline your product and gather AI-generated drafts.

Day 6–9: Design and format.

Day 10–11: Create mockups and descriptions.

Day 12: List on your chosen platform.

Day 13–14: Launch with a small promo campaign.

Services make money today. Digital products keep making money tomorrow. By combining AI's speed with evergreen product types, you can create assets that bring in revenue while you sleep — and build a portfolio that grows in value every time you release something new.

In the next chapter, we'll look at **Niche Media with AI** — how to use these same tools to build an audience that feeds your product sales without relying entirely on ads.

CHAPTER 17

Niche Media and Content Brands

If you want leverage in the digital world, own the attention. Service businesses make money by trading time for deliverables. Product businesses scale by selling the same thing repeatedly. But media businesses? They scale by building an audience — and then monetizing that audience in multiple ways.

A niche media brand is essentially an audience hub. It could be a blog, a YouTube channel, a newsletter, or all three working together. The keyword is niche — the tighter your focus, the easier it is to attract loyal followers and dominate a space.

AI can accelerate every step: researching the niche, creating the content, optimizing for search or algorithms, and repurposing material across formats.

M – Monetize via Platforms

M for Monetize via Platforms shows up again here. If you're building a niche content brand, YouTube, TikTok, or Substack can all be turned into revenue engines once you layer on ads, sponsorships, and products.

P – Publish & Promote

This chapter is also where the second P—Publish & Promote—comes alive. AI helps you push content faster, but publishing without promotion is like shouting into the void. Schedule, repurpose, and automate so your work travels.

Why Niche Media Works

Owning a niche media property means:

- You're not dependent on one client or one product.
- You can monetize in dozens of ways: ads, sponsorships, products, services, and affiliates.
- Your audience grows in value over time.

This is the opposite of chasing one-off sales. Instead, you're building an asset that compounds.

Choose a Niche You Can Own

Not "health" or "business" — those are too broad. Think **specific audience + specific interest**.

Examples:

- "Meal prep for busy nurses"
- "DIY home studio setup for podcasters"
- "Budget travel hacks for digital nomads"

Validation checklist:

Is there a large enough audience? (Search volume, social groups, forums). Are people spending money on it? (Courses, gear, software, events). Can you stand to talk about it for 100+ pieces of content?

AI prompt for niche research:

Give me 15 niche content ideas that combine [topic area] with [target audience]. Include audience size estimates, common pain points, and monetization possibilities.

Pick Your Primary Platform

Start with one core format you can commit to consistently, then branch out.

Blogs – Search-focused, evergreen traffic.

- Pros: Content can rank for years.
- Cons: Takes months to build traffic.
- AI role: Keyword research, article outlines, draft writing, SEO meta descriptions.

YouTube Channels – Algorithm-driven discovery.

- Pros: Video builds deep trust.
- Cons: Requires filming and editing.
- AI role: Scriptwriting, thumbnail ideas, title testing, captions.

Newsletters – Direct connection to your audience.

- Pros: You own the list, no algorithm dependency.
- Cons: Requires ongoing email creation.
- AI role: Issue ideas, copy editing, and automated segmentation emails.

Build a Content Plan That Doesn't Burn You Out

The biggest killer of niche media projects is inconsistency. AI can significantly reduce tedious tasks.

Example: Blog-based brand

- Use AI to research 50 long-tail keywords your audience searches for.
- Batch-generate outlines for all 50.
- Write or AI-draft 2–3 articles per week.

Example: YouTube-based brand

- Research 20 trending topics with AI (scrape video titles, summarize comments).
- Write five scripts in one sitting.
- Batch record.

Example: Newsletter-based brand

- Pick a consistent theme (weekly tips, curated industry news).
- Use AI to summarize articles, generate intro hooks, and format the issue.

Create a Repeatable Workflow

A good workflow means you can create content without starting from scratch each time.

Example **Blog Workflow**:

1. AI keyword research → select topic.

2. AI outline with headings, SEO targets.
3. AI draft → human polish.
4. AI meta description, image prompts for Midjourney.
5. Schedule in CMS.

Example **YouTube Workflow**:

1. AI trend research → pick three topics.
2. AI draft scripts.
3. Record + edit.
4. AI generates captions and social snippets.

Example **Newsletter Workflow**:

1. AI aggregates relevant links and stories.
2. AI drafts summaries and commentary.
3. Add personal notes and calls to action.

Monetization Paths for Niche Media

Once you have consistent traffic or subscribers, monetizing your content becomes easier.

Common income streams:

- Display ads (Google AdSense, Mediavine).
- Sponsorships (direct deals with brands).
- Affiliate marketing (earn % on recommended products).
- Selling your digital products or courses.

- Offering premium paid newsletter tiers.

Pro tip: Layer monetization. Don't just rely on ads. Combine 2–3 methods so one dip doesn't tank your revenue.

Repurpose Like a Machine

One of the most potent advantages of AI is turning one core piece of content into multiple others.

Example: You record a 10-minute YouTube video.

- AI → turns script into a blog article.
- AI → generates a newsletter summary.
- AI → pulls three short clips for TikTok/Instagram.

This keeps your brand everywhere without tripling your workload.

Grow Faster with AI-Assisted SEO and Algorithm Tuning

For blogs:

- AI can cluster related keywords into topic hubs.
- AI can optimize internal linking structures.

For YouTube:

- AI can test different title + thumbnail variations.
- AI can analyze retention graphs and suggest edits.

For newsletters:

- AI can segment your audience by click patterns.

- AI can A/B test subject lines.

Build a Brand, Not Just a Content Feed

A niche content brand feels intentional — not random posts scattered around.

Brand elements:

- A clear voice and tone.
- Consistent visuals (colors, fonts, imagery style).
- A recognizable hook or tagline.

AI role:

- Help define your brand's voice guide.
- Generate a bank of taglines and slogans.
- Suggest content pillars that align with your identity.

Case Study: Newsletter to Media Business in 6 Months

A solo marketer started a weekly "AI Tools Roundup" email.

- Month 1: 200 subscribers from LinkedIn posts.
- Month 3: AI-assisted content allowed her to send twice a week without burnout.
- Month 4: Added affiliate links to featured tools.
- Month 6: 5,000 subscribers, $1,500/month from affiliates, $750/month from one sponsor.

The turning point wasn't just about content volume — it was about building a habit for her readers and establishing a repeatable system for herself.

Pitfalls to Avoid

- **Starting too broad.** The temptation is to appeal to everyone. You'll get lost.
- **Content without distribution.** A blog without an SEO plan or a YouTube channel without outreach won't grow.
- **Relying only on AI output.** It needs your personality and insights to stand out.

Quick Start Plan: Launch Your Niche Media Brand in 30 Days

Week 1: Choose your niche and platform.

Week 2: Set up your brand assets and create 10 content ideas with AI.

Week 3: Produce and schedule 5–7 pieces.

Week 4: Launch with a light promotion push and start gathering feedback.

Niche media is one of the few online plays that compounds in value. Every post, video, or email is a brick in a structure you can monetize in endless ways. With AI, you can build that structure faster, more consistently, and with less overhead than ever before.

In the next chapter, we'll explore **Agency-Lite Automations** — how to scale your reach and revenue by using AI systems to handle most of the heavy lifting without becoming a bloated, high-overhead agency.

CHAPTER 18

Agency-Lite Automations

Running a traditional agency can be rewarding — but it can also be a grind. Full-time staff, constant client calls, scope creep, and unpredictable workloads can leave you feeling more like a firefighter than a business owner.

Agency-lite flips the model. Instead of scaling through hiring and billable hours, you scale through repeatable, AI-powered workflows. You still deliver value to clients, but you do it with lean systems, minimal overhead, and predictable margins.

This chapter is about how to package your AI skills into client-ready services that run like clockwork.

M – Monetize via Platforms

The M step—Monetize via Platforms—takes a different shape here. Instead of selling products, you're building systems that clients pay for. Automations delivered through Zapier, Notion, or Airtable can become subscription-style revenue streams.

What Makes It "Agency-Lite"

- **Lean team (or solo)** – You don't need an army of account managers.
- **Pre-defined services** – No endless custom proposals.

- **Automated delivery** – Systems do most of the heavy lifting.
- **Predictable pricing** – You know exactly how much time and cost are involved.

It's not about being small — it's about being streamlined.

Pick Services That Automate Well

Not every service is a good fit. Look for things that:

- Have a transparent, repeatable process.
- Produce a tangible, consistent deliverable.
- It can be at least 50% automated without sacrificing quality.

High-fit examples:

- Monthly blog content packages.
- Social media post creation and scheduling.
- Email newsletter production.
- Podcast show notes and transcriptions.
- Market research reports.
- SEO audits and keyword lists.

Low-fit examples:

- Open-ended strategy consulting (too custom).
- Complex creative branding projects (too subjective).

Map the Workflow Before Selling It

The temptation is to sell first, figure it out later. But with agency-lite, your profit margin depends on knowing exactly how you'll deliver before you take a client on.

Example: "Monthly Blog Content" service.

1. **Client intake** – Form to gather topics, keywords, and tone.
2. **AI outline** – Generate headings and key points.
3. **AI draft** – Write 1,000–1,200 words.
4. **Human edit** – Quick review and polish.
5. **Image generation** – Midjourney for custom visuals.
6. **Publish** – Upload to CMS, schedule social promo.

Every step is documented. Anyone can follow it. That's how you scale without losing control.

Build the Automation Stack

You don't have to automate everything — but the more you automate, the more clients you can handle without stress.

Tools to consider:

- **ChatGPT, Claude, Gemini** – Content generation, research, summarization.
- **Zapier / Make** – Connect apps and trigger workflows automatically.

- **Airtable / Notion** – Track client projects and store deliverables.
- **Buffer / Publer** – Schedule social media content.
- **Fathom / Otter.ai** – Auto-transcribe and summarize calls.

Example automation:

1. New client submits intake form (Typeform).
2. Zapier sends details to Airtable and triggers AI to generate the first outline.
3. AI draft reviewed in Google Docs.
4. On approval, Zapier schedules the post in WordPress and sends a "Your content is ready" email to the client.

Productize Your Pricing

One of the most significant stress points in agency life is *custom quotes*. Agency-lite skips that.

Productized pricing means:

- A fixed deliverable.
- A fixed turnaround time.
- A fixed price.

Example:

- "4 blog posts/month, SEO-optimized, with images" – $600/month.

- "12 Instagram posts with captions and hashtags" – $450/month.
- "Monthly market trends report" – $350/month.

Clients know what they're getting. You know exactly how much work is involved.

Set Realistic Turnarounds

Automation makes things fast, but don't promise "instant." Build in a buffer for human review and client feedback.

Pro tip: For monthly services, set a cut-off date for content requests so you can batch work and deliver on schedule.

Build a Simple Client Onboarding

Keep onboarding friction low.

- **Welcome email** – Explains the process and expectations.
- **Intake form** – One place to collect all necessary info.
- **Kickoff checklist** – So clients feel confident you're organized.

AI can even help write onboarding guides that sound polished and personal.

Manage Client Communication Like a Pro

Agency-lite thrives on boundaries.

- Use a single communication channel (email or Slack, not both).
- Set clear response times.

- Send progress updates at predictable intervals.

AI can help here too — drafting polite follow-ups, summarizing threads, and preparing quick status reports.

Sell the Outcome, Not the Method

Clients don't care if you use AI or a typewriter. They care about the result.

Instead of: "We use AI to create your blog posts."

Say: "We deliver consistent, well-researched, and SEO-optimized blog posts every month without you having to write a word."

The method is your advantage — but it's not the selling point.

Layer in Upsells and Add-Ons

Once your core workflow is running smoothly, you can add profitable extras:

- Extra posts or videos.
- SEO keyword packs.
- Quarterly analytics reports.
- Repurposing content into other formats.

Because your base process is already automated, upsells are easy to fulfill.

Example: Agency-Lite in Action

Service: "Weekly LinkedIn Content for Coaches"

Workflow:

1. Monday – Client uploads voice note with weekly topic.
2. AI transcribes and creates three post drafts.
3. Human reviews, tweaks tone, schedules in Buffer.
4. Friday – Send client a "week in review" email with performance stats.

Results:

- One person manages 12 clients in ~8 hours/week.
- 85% gross margin.
- Clients stay an average of 9 months.

Scaling Without the Chaos

The beauty of agency-lite is that you can scale without burning out.

- Add more clients → automate more steps.
- Hire contractors for the human review step if needed.
- Keep your service menu tight — 3–5 offerings max.

Pitfalls to Avoid

- **Customizing too much per client.** Every exception adds complexity.
- **Selling before testing.** Make sure your workflow works with dummy projects first.
- **Over-promising AI capabilities.** Set expectations honestly.

Quick Start Plan: Launch Your First Agency-Lite Offer in 21 Days

Week 1:

- Pick a repeatable, automatable service.
- Map your exact workflow.

Week 2:

- Build automation steps.
- Price and package the offer.

Week 3:

- Onboard 1–2 test clients.
- Refine based on real delivery experience.

Agency-lite isn't about being small — it's about being smart. You're packaging value in a way that's repeatable, scalable, and profitable without adding unnecessary complexity.

In the next chapter, we'll get into **Pricing and Simple Unit Economics** — because knowing exactly what a service costs to deliver is the key to keeping margins healthy as you grow.

CHAPTER 19

Pricing and Simple Unit Economics

If you want to run a business that lasts, you need to know two numbers cold:

1. What do you charge?
2. What does it cost you to deliver?

Everything else — marketing, branding, scaling — depends on getting those two right.

This chapter strips pricing and unit economics down to their core. By the time you finish, you'll know how to set a price that makes sense, track your margins, and scale without watching profit disappear.

T – Track & Tweak for Profit

Here's the T in PROMPT: Track & Tweak for Profit. Pricing isn't set-and-forget. Track sales data, tweak offers, and test bundles. AI can crunch numbers, but the profit comes from you making decisions with that feedback.

Why Pricing Is More Than Just a Number

Too many people pick prices based on what "feels fair" or what their competitors charge. That's backwards. Your price should be built on:

- Your costs (time, tools, labor).
- The value to the customer.
- The margin you need to grow.

If you don't know your numbers, you can grow your business and still go broke.

Understand Your Unit Economics

Unit economics means the financials of delivering one unit of your service or product.

If you sell "4 blog posts/month" as a package:

- One unit = one month of that package for one client.

Your goal is to know:

- Revenue per unit.
- Cost per unit.
- Profit per unit.

Example:

- Price: $600/month.
- AI tool subscriptions: $30/month (allocated per client).
- Your time: 4 hours/month at $50/hour = $200.
- Total cost: $230.
- Profit: $370.
- Margin: 61%.

That's a healthy margin. But if you only clear 20% or less, scaling will be complex without cutting costs or raising prices.

Break Down Your Costs

Costs aren't just your software subscriptions. Include:

- **Direct labor** – your hours or contractor pay.
- **AI tool costs** – pro plan fees, API calls, cloud storage.
- **Assets** – stock photos, templates.
- **Payment processing fees** – usually 2–4%.
- **Other overhead** – hosting, email platform, project management tools.

Pro tip: For services, time is your most significant cost. Even if you're not paying yourself yet, assign a dollar value to your hours. Otherwise, you'll underprice.

Pick a Pricing Model

The best model depends on the type of product or service:

Flat rate (productized services)

- Predictable for you and the client.
- Example: $450/month for 12 Instagram posts.

Per deliverable

- Good if work volume fluctuates.
- Example: $150/blog post.

Tiered packages

- Let's let our clients choose based on budget.
- Example: Basic ($450), Pro ($750), Premium ($1,200).

Performance-based

- There's a high upside if you can track the results.
- Example: 10% of ad spend + performance bonus.

Factor in Value, Not Just Cost

Pricing isn't only math — it's also perception.

Example: If your AI workflow saves a company 20 hours/month, and their team bills $100/hour, you've delivered $2,000 in value. Charging $500/month for that is a no-brainer. Ask: What is this worth to the client if it works exactly as promised?

Avoid the Race to the Bottom

AI tools enable faster and cheaper delivery. But don't fall into the trap of competing only on price.

Instead of being "the cheapest," be:

- The most reliable.
- The most specialized.
- The one with the fastest turnaround.

This is where niching down pays off — specialists command higher rates.

Track Margins Monthly

Margins can erode quietly. Your AI tool usage spikes, or you start spending more time per client than planned.

Use a simple tracker (Google Sheets, Airtable, Notion) to monitor:

- Client name.
- Package price.
- Hours spent.
- Direct costs.
- Profit per month.

If a client's margin drops below your target, decide:

- Raise their price.
- Adjust scope.
- Let them go.

Build in Scalability From the Start

A business that can't handle more clients without breaking is just a job with extra paperwork.

To scale profitably:

- Standardize your deliverables.
- Automate as much as possible.
- Document your processes so you can hand them off.

If your "unit" currently takes 4 hours, your goal is to reduce it to 2 hours without compromising quality. That doubles your potential client load without raising costs.

Price Testing Without Risking Your Whole Client Base

You don't have to overhaul prices for everyone at once. Try:

- Raising rates for new clients first.
- Offering "add-ons" instead of raising the core price.
- Creating a premium tier for those who want faster delivery or extra features.

If the higher price sells easily, you've been undercharging.

Use AI to Help Price Smart

AI can't decide your value for you, but it can help with:

- Competitor price analysis (scraping and summarizing data).
- Profit simulations ("If costs go up 15%, what's my new break-even price?").
- Proposal drafting with precise ROI calculations.

Prompt: Based on this service description and cost breakdown, suggest three price points: low, mid, and premium, with justifications for each.

Know Your Breakeven Point

Your breakeven point is the number of units you need to sell to cover all fixed costs.

Example:

- Fixed costs/month: $3,000.
- Profit per unit: $300.
- Breakeven: 10 clients/month.

Anything beyond that is pure profit (minus taxes). This indicates how aggressive your marketing strategy needs to be.

Mini Case Study: From Guesswork to Predictable Profit

Before tracking unit economics, a freelance marketer charged $200 for each blog post. After calculating:

- Time spent: 4 hours.
- Hourly rate goal: $50/hour.
- AI tools: $20/post.
- Profit: $180, but the margin is only 45%.

She raised her price to $300/post, cut production time to 2.5 hours using AI, and now earns $230/post at a 77% margin. She also works fewer hours for the same income.

Standard Pricing Mistakes to Avoid

- **Basing the price only on competitors.** Their costs may be lower — or they may be losing money.
- **Ignoring your time.** It's still a cost, even if you "don't mind doing it."
- **Not raising prices.** Inflation hits software fees and labor, too.

- **Bundling too much.** Every extra feature eats margin unless it's priced in.

Quick Start Plan: Set Profitable Pricing in 7 Days

Day 1: List your direct and indirect costs.

Day 2: Calculate hours per unit.

Day 3: Decide on your target margin.

Day 4: Build a cost + margin price point.

Day 5: Compare with competitor rates for positioning.

Day 6: Write clear package descriptions.

Day 7: Start selling at the new rate to new clients.

Reasonable pricing isn't about squeezing the most money out of a client — it's about making sure your business is healthy enough to serve them well over the long haul. When you know your unit economics, you make decisions with clarity instead of guesswork.

In the next chapter, we'll close out the monetization section by exploring **Career Paths in the AI Economy** — from solo operator to media owner to platform builder.

PART V

Level Up

At this point, you've got the foundations, the workflows, the reliability layer, and the monetization paths. Part V is about taking everything you've built and moving it up a level—so you don't just make money once, but keep growing your skills, your reputation, and your income.

Here's what's ahead:

- **Chapter 20** explores *Career Paths in the AI Era*. Whether you're building your own brand or slotting AI into an existing role, this is where you learn how to position yourself in a market that's moving fast.
- **Chapter 21** covers *Portfolio Projects That Open Doors*, because showing your work is often more powerful than talking about it.
- **Chapter 22** closes with an *Ongoing Learning Checklist*, giving you a practical way to stay sharp while the tech keeps evolving.

This is where the second P in PROMPT—Publish & Promote—comes into focus.

Publishing is more than just hitting "post." It's about putting your work into the world, consistently, in places where it can be seen. Promotion isn't about hype—it's about distribution. If you build AI-driven projects but keep them private, they don't create opportunities. If you publish them, share them, and promote them, they become magnets for clients, employers, or collaborators.

And here's where T-Track & Tweak for Profit loops back in. Publishing is half the job; tracking the response is the other half. Which portfolio pieces get attention? Which posts get shared? Which offers get clicks? By measuring, you learn. By tweaking, you grow.

Part V is about turning your AI skills into visible, market-ready assets. It's about treating your career or business like a living system—always learning, always shipping, constantly improving. That's how you level up, and that's how you make sure the PROMPT Goldmine System™ doesn't just help you start—it enables you to keep winning long after you finish this book.

CHAPTER 20

Career Paths in the AI Era

Careers aren't static anymore. The old "get a degree, work 30 years, retire" model is gone. In its place is a dynamic landscape where new roles emerge almost overnight — especially in artificial intelligence. The people who thrive now are the ones who can see where things are going and position themselves ahead of the curve.

This chapter looks at the most viable career paths in the AI era, how to transition into them, and what it takes to make AI a central part of your work.

P – Position Your Niche

Remember the P in PROMPT: Position Your Niche. The same principle applies to your career. Don't brand yourself as a generic 'AI consultant.' Narrow down—AI for lawyers, AI for real estate, AI for wellness—and suddenly you're the obvious choice for clients in that lane.

The AI Career Shift Is Already Here

You've probably seen the headlines: "AI will replace jobs." That's true in one sense — repetitive, rules-based work is being automated. But it's also creating new categories of work we didn't have five years ago.

Here's the bigger truth: AI isn't replacing all jobs. It's replacing certain specific inside jobs. People who learn to work with AI will replace those who don't.

Decide If You Want to Go All-In or Hybrid

There are two broad paths you can take:

- **All-In AI Roles** – Your core job is AI-focused. You're building models, creating workflows, training systems, or selling AI-powered solutions.
- **Hybrid Roles** – You stay in your existing field but use AI to boost results, productivity, and earnings.

Both paths work. The "all-in" route is more of a career pivot. The hybrid route lets you upgrade what you're already doing.

AI Career Path #1: Prompt Engineering and Workflow Design

If AI models are the engines, prompts are the steering wheel. Prompt engineers understand how to structure instructions so AI produces reliable, high-quality output.

Skills needed:

- Understanding model strengths and weaknesses.
- Writing structured, unambiguous prompts.
- Building repeatable templates and workflows.

Earning potential:

- Freelancers: $50–$200/hour.
- Corporate roles: $80k–$150k/year.

Entry strategy:

- Build a portfolio of working prompts and show before/after results.
- Offer small gigs on marketplaces like Fiverr, Contra, or Upwork to build credibility.

AI Career Path #2: AI Product Creator

This path involves packaging AI capabilities into paid products, such as tools, templates, or content packs, for sale.

Examples:

- Notion dashboards with AI-assisted automation.
- Midjourney prompt packs for niche industries.
- AI-powered spreadsheet templates.

Skills needed:

- Creativity in applying AI to real problems.
- Light coding or no-code tools like Zapier, Make, or Bubble.
- Marketing and distribution.

Earning potential:

- $1k–$10k/month for niche products with steady sales.

AI Career Path #3: AI Consultant for Businesses

Small businesses recognize the importance of AI but are unsure where to begin. This is where consultants step in.

Typical work:

- Audit the business to find automation opportunities.
- Set up AI tools for marketing, operations, or customer service.
- Train teams to use the systems.

Skills needed:

- Broad understanding of AI tools.
- Ability to map tech to business needs.
- Communication and training ability.

Earning potential:

- $100–$250/hour.
- Retainers of $1k–$5k/month for ongoing support.

AI Career Path #4: Data and Insight Specialist

Data is AI's raw material. Specialists collect, clean, and interpret it so organizations can make better decisions.

Roles include:

- Data labeling and annotation.
- Data analysis with AI-assisted tools.
- Business intelligence reporting.

Skills needed:

- Excel, Google Sheets, SQL basics.

- Familiarity with AI data tools (Tableau, Power BI, ChatGPT for analysis).

Earning potential:

- Entry-level: $50k–$70k/year.
- Experienced: $90k–$130k/year.

AI Career Path #5: Content Creator Powered by AI

This blends creativity with automation. You build an audience on YouTube, TikTok, newsletters, or blogs — but AI handles much of the heavy lifting.

AI assists with:

- Topic research.
- Scriptwriting or article drafts.
- Graphic and video asset creation.

Monetization options:

- Ads and sponsorships.
- Affiliate marketing.
- Selling digital products.

Earning potential:

- $500/month hobby → $10k+/month for established brands.

AI Career Path #6: AI in Specialized Professions

Every industry now has room for AI specialists:

- Law: AI-assisted case research.
- Healthcare: Patient record analysis, diagnostic support.
- Real estate: Market trend forecasting.
- Education: AI-driven tutoring systems.

You don't need to leave your field — just become the person who knows how to apply AI inside it.

Transitioning Into an AI Role Without Starting Over

Not everyone can (or wants to) go back to school or quit their job cold. The more brilliant play is to transition in phases.

Phase 1: Start using AI in your current role to improve output.

Track your results.

Phase 2: Build side projects or a portfolio showing your AI work.

Phase 3: Offer small paid services to test the market.

Phase 4: Expand into a full-time role or business if demand is strong.

The Skills You Can't Skip

Regardless of the path, these skills matter:

1. Prompting and workflow design – You need to speak "AI" fluently.
2. Critical thinking – AI will give you confident but wrong answers. You need to spot them.

3. Tool adaptability – Today's best tool may not exist in six months.

4. Basic data literacy – Understanding how to interpret and work with data is a superpower.

5. Soft skills – Clients and employers still value clear communication, reliability, and problem-solving.

Using AI to Find AI Jobs

AI can help you break into AI. Examples:

- Summarize dozens of job postings to find common skills.
- Rewrite your resume in the language hiring managers look for.
- Prepare for interviews with AI-generated practice questions.

Prompt example: Analyze these five job postings and tell me the top 10 skills and phrases I should highlight on my resume.

Freelance vs. Employment in AI

Freelance pros:

- Freedom to choose clients and projects.
- Higher earning ceiling if you can scale.

Freelance cons:

- No guaranteed income.
- You handle sales, admin, and delivery.

Employment pros:

- Steady paycheck.
- The company covers tools and training.

Employment cons:

- Less control over projects.
- Salary caps, unless you change roles.

Many people start freelancing on the side, then decide later whether to go all-in.

Case Study: From Teacher to AI Consultant

Sarah, a high school teacher, started using ChatGPT to plan lessons. She posted examples on LinkedIn and got messages from small business owners asking if she could "do that AI thing" for them. She took on two clients, used weekends to build their automation systems, and within eight months was making more from AI consulting than teaching. She transitioned full time without going broke.

The Long Game: Future-Proofing Your AI Career

AI is evolving fast. Today's hot skill could be commoditized tomorrow. The way to stay ahead:

- Continue to build your adaptability by learning new tools regularly.
- Own your audience or network so opportunities come to you.
- Focus on transferable skills like analysis, communication, and decision-making.

Quick Start Plan: Build Your AI Career in 90 Days

Month 1: Learn core tools (ChatGPT, Midjourney, one automation tool).

Month 2: Apply them in a portfolio project or side gig.

Month 3: Publish your work online, network with others in your chosen niche, and pitch for your first paid opportunity.

The AI era isn't about replacing people with machines — it's about replacing people who don't know how to use machines with those who do. Whether you go all-in on an AI-focused role or use AI to supercharge your existing career, the opportunity is wide open.

In the next chapter, we'll shift gears into **Portfolio Projects** — practical builds that show you can walk the talk and make you stand out to clients and employers alike.

CHAPTER 21

Portfolio Projects That Open Doors

If a resume tells people what you've done, a portfolio shows them what you can do.

In the AI era, this matters more than ever. Hiring managers, clients, and collaborators don't just want to hear about your skills — they want proof you can apply them.

A portfolio project isn't just something you make for fun. Done right, it's a sales tool, a conversation starter, and a credibility booster all in one. This chapter will show you how to design projects that get noticed, even if you have no formal AI job experience yet.

Why Portfolio Projects Work So Well in AI

AI is still a fast-moving space. There are no decades-old credentials or standardized pathways into most AI-related roles. That means a publicly visible project can sometimes beat a traditional qualification.

A good portfolio project:

- **Demonstrates skill** — People can see you know what you're doing.

- **Proves initiative** — You didn't wait for someone to assign the work.
- **Stays relevant** — You can update it to reflect the latest tools.
- **Builds trust** — Shows you can take an idea from concept to delivery.

Think of it as your "practice field" where you can experiment and still come out looking professional.

Pick the Right Type of Project

Not all portfolio projects have the same impact.

The sweet spot is where your interests, skills, and the target audience's needs overlap. Here are examples by goal:

For business consulting roles:

- Automating a small business's email follow-up process.
- AI-generated market research reports.

For creative/content roles:

- An AI-assisted YouTube channel with original scripts and visuals.
- A blog series where each post uses a different AI-powered workflow.

For data/analysis roles:

- A dashboard pulling in live data and AI-generated summaries.

- A "data cleanup challenge" where you show before/after results.

Start Small but Show the Whole Process

Your project doesn't have to be massive. A polished, well-documented small project beats a half-finished giant one.

Include these in your project presentation:

Problem statement – What problem are you solving?

Tools used – Which AI models, APIs, or platforms?

Your process – Screenshots, workflows, and step-by-step explanations.

The result – Final output, metrics, or before/after comparisons.

Reflection – What you'd improve or try next.

This gives your audience a narrative to follow, not just a finished product.

Make It Relevant to the Role You Want

If you want to land AI marketing gigs, don't make your portfolio all about AI for video game development. Tailor your projects to match the field.

Applying for a social media strategist role? Show an AI workflow that:

- Generates a month of posts from one content source.
- Creates platform-specific captions and hashtags.

- Schedules them automatically.

When your portfolio matches the employer's world, it's easier for them to imagine you on the team.

Use Realistic Constraints

A lot of AI "demo" projects are flashy but unrealistic — they rely on perfect inputs, ignore budget limits, or require manual steps that aren't scalable.

If you want to impress serious clients or employers:

- Use realistic datasets or prompts.
- Document costs (API usage, subscriptions).
- Build in error handling or checks.

This demonstrates your ability to think like someone delivering in the real world, not just in a controlled sandbox.

Document Like a Teacher

Imagine your project will be used as a tutorial. That mindset forces you to:

- Explain each decision.
- Show your testing process.
- Note what didn't work.

Employers love this because it shows how you think, not just what you made.

Publish It Publicly

Don't hide your portfolio away in a folder only you can see. Publish it on platforms where your target audience hangs out:

- **GitHub** – Great for technical projects and workflow code.
- **Notion or Google Docs** – For process write-ups and case studies.
- **LinkedIn** – For showcasing before/after results and engaging in discussions.
- **Your site** – A hub for all projects, easy to send in a single link.

The goal is to make it findable. Someone searching your name should quickly find examples of your work.

Keep a "Live" Portfolio

AI tools change fast. A stale portfolio from 2022 won't impress in today's world. Set a reminder to update or replace old projects every 3–6 months.

One way to keep it fresh is to document your learning — post short write-ups on new AI workflows you're testing. Even if they're not complete projects, they keep you visible.

Add Metrics Where Possible

Results speak louder than features. If your AI social media workflow increased engagement, say by how much.

Examples:

- "Cut content creation time from 5 hours to 45 minutes."

- "Generated 12% higher email open rates."
- "Reduced customer support backlog by 30%."

Metrics turn a cool project into a compelling business case.

Borrow Credibility (Ethically)

You can build projects for real businesses (with permission) or partner with friends who have active ventures.

Example: Offer to create an AI-powered marketing campaign for a local coffee shop in exchange for using the results in your portfolio. It's a win-win: they get free help, you get a live case study.

Stack Projects for Impact

One project shows you can execute. Three or four show you're consistent.

Aim for:

- 1 showcase project – Your most impressive, relevant work.
- 2–3 supporting projects – Smaller, varied examples.

This gives depth without overwhelming someone reviewing your portfolio.

Sample Project Ideas by Category

Business & Productivity:

- An AI assistant that manages meeting notes, action items, and follow-ups.

- Sales lead scoring system using AI and CRM data.

Creative & Media:

- AI-generated short film with script, voiceover, and visuals.
- A podcast series where AI helps with research, editing, and promotion.

Data & Analysis:

- Industry trend report compiled from public sources with AI summaries.
- The competitor analysis dashboard is updated weekly by automation.

Turning a Project Into an Opportunity

The project itself is only part of the play. The other half is telling the right people about it.

Steps to promote without feeling spammy:

1. Post a short case study on LinkedIn or Twitter.
2. Share behind-the-scenes process videos on TikTok or YouTube.
3. Email a select list of potential clients or employers with the link and a short note on how it could apply to them.

Case Study: How One Project Landed a Six-Figure Role

Mark, a freelance writer, sought to break into the field of AI content strategy. He built a public Notion dashboard that used AI to:

- Pull trending keywords.
- Generate blog outlines.
- Schedule social promotion.

He posted a walkthrough video on LinkedIn. It got 12,000 views and a comment from a SaaS founder who later hired him as head of content automation — at triple his previous rate.

Pitfalls to Avoid

- **Copying tutorials exactly** – Add your twist, or you'll blend in with everyone else.
- **Overcomplicating it** – Don't build something so fragile it only works once.
- **Hiding the human input** – Show where you made decisions, not just AI outputs.

Quick Start Plan: Build Your First AI Portfolio Project in 30 Days

Week 1: Pick a problem worth solving and sketch the workflow.

Week 2: Build the core system using AI + supporting tools.

Week 3: Test, refine, and collect screenshots/results.

Week 4: Publish the project with a write-up and share it.

A portfolio project is more than a side experiment — it's a public proof of skill, a way to start conversations, and a door-opener to bigger opportunities. In AI, where the tools and roles evolve quickly, your portfolio becomes a living, breathing asset that keeps you relevant.

In the next chapter, we'll close with **Ongoing Learning in AI** — how to stay sharp without drowning in constant updates.

Chapter 22

Ongoing Learning Checklist

Learning AI is not like learning a programming language once and calling it a day. It's like being in an ocean where the tide shifts daily. New tools emerge, old ones fade, prices change, features move. If you don't have a plan for ongoing learning, you'll either get overwhelmed or slowly drift behind.

The goal of this chapter is to give you a repeatable system — something you can run in the background of your life so you stay current without letting "keeping up" become your full-time job.

P – Publish & Promote

Remember the P in PROMPT: Publish & Promote. Continuous learning is only half the equation—you also must share what you're building. Publish your experiments, promote your wins, and you'll stay top of mind in your niche.

Why Ongoing Learning Matters More in AI

AI isn't a static field. It's an evolving ecosystem that blends computer science, business models, ethics, and human behavior. That means:

- **Skills depreciate faster** – What worked last year may not work today.

- **Opportunities pop up unexpectedly** – Being first matters.
- **Regulations change** – You need to know the rules before they bite you.
- **Competition is global** – You're not just competing with your local market anymore.

If you want to stay relevant — whether as a freelancer, employee, or business owner — you need a learning habit that keeps your skills sharp without chaining you to your screen.

Principle #1: Follow Streams, Not Floods

The biggest mistake is trying to follow *everything*. Instead, choose a few **streams** of information you trust.

Example setup:

- **1–2 high-signal newsletters** (e.g., Ben's Bites, The Rundown AI).
- **1–2 YouTube channels** focused on tutorials in your niche.
- **1 community** (Reddit, Discord, or LinkedIn group) where peers share real experiences.

Anything more than that and you'll start spending more time consuming than creating.

Principle #2: Use a "Learn-Apply-Teach" Cycle

Information sticks when you:

Learn – Read/watch the new concept.

Apply – Use it in a small project immediately.

Teach – Explain it to someone else (or post about it online).

Even if you don't have an audience, writing a LinkedIn post or short Loom video explaining what you learned forces clarity. And it positions you as someone active in the space.

Principle #3: Capture, Don't Chase

Instead of trying to "keep up" daily, capture resources into a **learning inbox** — a Notion board, Google Doc, or even a Trello list — and review them weekly.

Why this works:

- Stops the constant mental tug of "I should read that now."
- Allows you to batch learn in focused sessions.
- Makes it easy to spot patterns in what's worth your time.

Principle #4: Pick a Focus Area Each Quarter

AI is too broad to master all at once. Every 90 days, choose a primary focus (e.g., AI for marketing automation, or AI data analysis) and go deeper there.

You'll keep an eye on big-picture developments, but your deep learning will be in a narrow lane — which builds actual expertise.

Principle #5: Build Relationships, Not Just Skills

Tools will change. Relationships last. Join a niche Slack group, local meetup, or online forum where you can:

- Ask real-world questions.
- See how others solve problems.
- Get early heads-up on opportunities.

Some of the best learning comes from *conversations*, not tutorials.

The Ongoing Learning Checklist

Here's a practical, no-fluff checklist you can run monthly and quarterly to keep yourself updated.

Monthly Tasks

Review your learning inbox

- Process saved articles, videos, or posts.
- Discard anything outdated or irrelevant.

Test 1–2 new tools

- Try them on a real project, even if small.
- Note pros/cons and whether they replace something you use.

Update one portfolio project

- Refresh with new workflows, features, or data.
- Shows you're active and evolving.

Share 1 insight publicly

- Post a short takeaway from your experiments.
- Keeps you visible without forcing you into daily posting.

Check costs

- Review AI tool subscriptions and API spend.
- Cancel or downgrade anything unused.

Quarterly Tasks

Pick a new focus area

- Decide what skill or domain you'll deepen next.

Archive old tools

- If something hasn't been used in 90 days, remove it from your active stack.

Refresh your knowledge base

- Update SOPs, prompt libraries, and automation scripts.

Benchmark your workflows

- Compare speed, cost, and quality with last quarter's results.

Attend one event

- Could be virtual or in-person. The goal is to expose oneself to fresh thinking.

Managing the Overwhelm Factor

Even with a checklist, the flood of AI updates can be overwhelming. Here's how to cut through it:

- Time-box your learning – e.g., 90 minutes on Friday afternoons.

- Ignore "shiny tool" FOMO unless it directly serves your current focus area.
- Unfollow low-signal sources – if a feed is more hype than substance, drop it.

Remember: You don't need to know everything. Just need to know enough to execute well in your lane.

Tools to Help You Stay Updated Without Drowning

- Feedly – Aggregate AI news from trusted sources.
- Readwise Reader – Save and resurface the most valuable content.
- Notion – Maintain your prompt library, workflow docs, and notes.
- Zapier/Make – Automate the capture of interesting links to your learning inbox.

How to Spot Real Shifts vs. Noise

Not every AI update is worth your attention. Train yourself to ask:

- Does this change what's possible in my work?
- Does it create a new opportunity or kill an old one?
- Will my clients/audience care?

If the answer is "no" three times, skip it.

Case Study: The "One Hour Friday" Rule

James, a freelance AI automation builder, stays sharp with a strict routine:

- Saves interesting AI updates to Notion all week.
- Every Friday from 3:00 to 4:00 pm, I review them.
- Tries one thing on a live client project.
- Write a short LinkedIn post about the result.

It's just one hour, but over 18 months, it's kept him ahead of 90% of his peers — and brought in clients who follow his posts.

Ethics and Long-Term Thinking

Part of learning responsibly is staying aware of:

- Bias in AI outputs.
- Privacy in data handling.
- Copyright in generated content.

Set reminders to revisit your stance on these as regulations and norms change. The last thing you want is to learn a workflow deeply only to find it's no longer legally usable.

Building a Learning Habit That Sticks

The trick isn't motivation — it's structure.

- Anchor learning to something you already do (e.g., right after morning coffee).
- Keep a visible tracker so you see your streak.

- Reward yourself for consistency, not just results.

Quick Start: Your First 30 Days of Ongoing Learning

Week 1: Pick your info streams and set up a learning inbox.

Week 2: Test one new tool and document your impressions.

Week 3: Join a relevant online group and participate once.

Week 4: Publish one short insight or tutorial.

By the end of the month, you'll have your system in motion — and it'll feel manageable.

Ongoing learning in AI isn't about chasing every shiny update. It's about building a lean, repeatable system that keeps you informed, sharp, and relevant — without stealing time from doing the work.

If you follow the checklist, you'll be positioned to adapt quickly, spot opportunities early, and avoid the burnout that takes out so many talented people in this space.

Appendices

You've reached the extras—the practical add-ons that give you even more ways to make money with AI. In these appendices, you'll find:

- **Over 100 Ways to Make Money with AI** — a big list to spark ideas you might not have considered.
- **Recommended Tools & Resources** — so you know what to use and where to start without wasting time.
- **Thank You** — because this is more than just a book; it's a system, and I'm glad you chose to put it in your hands.

Here's the thing: the appendices aren't just "bonus reading." They connect back to the PROMPT Goldmine System™ one last time.

- If you're still working on **Position Your Niche**, the "100 Ways" list is gold—you'll see dozens of possible angles to explore.
- If you're focused on **Research Winning Content**, the tools and resources appendix will give you fresh ways to gather data and test ideas.

- If you want to **Optimize with AI**, the tool list will point you toward platforms that make the process smoother.
- If you're ready to **Monetize via Platforms**, the examples in the "100 Ways" list will show you exactly where to plug in.
- For **Publish & Promote**, the resources can help you distribute, schedule, and automate so you get visibility.
- And for **Track & Tweak for Profit**, use these appendices as a living reference—come back when you're stuck or need to adjust your strategy.

Think of the appendices as your **continuation kit.** The chapters gave you the playbook. PROMPT gave you the system. The appendices are what you'll use to refresh your ideas, grab new tools, and keep building long after you've closed the book.

Over 100 Ways to Make Money With AI

One of AI's best sites for finding new AI Tools is theresanaiforthat.com. Discover the latest and newest tools to captivate your interest. Please bookmark this site for future searches, as it's a treasure trove of invaluable resources.

Key markers:

💰 = Fast ROI

🕒 = Low Time Investment

📈 = Scalable Long-Term

How to Use This Appendix

This section is more than just a big list. It's a menu of money-making opportunities sorted into categories. Your goal isn't to do everything. Your goal is to pick one or two that match your skills, resources, and time, then get them live quickly.

Think of it like a restaurant menu — skimming every option is fine, but eventually you've got to choose and place your order.

Step 1 — Scan by Category

Look for the categories that fit your background. A marketer will feel at home in the AI Marketing section. A spreadsheet whiz might gravitate toward AI Data Cleanup.

Step 2 — Choose Your Starting Point

From your chosen category, pick just one idea you could launch in the next 30 days. Ignore the temptation to "stack" multiple offers until the first one is running smoothly.

Step 3 — Make It Specific

The more targeted your offer, the faster you'll get traction.

- Instead of "AI blog writing," do "AI-written blog posts for fitness coaches."
- Instead of "AI image generation," do "Midjourney book covers for self-published authors."

Step 4 — Price and Package It

Decide if you'll charge per project, per hour, or as a retainer. Even a $100/month service with 10 clients is $1,000/month.

Step 5 — Launch Fast, Improve Later

Don't over-engineer your setup. Start with simple tools, basic marketing, and direct outreach. Then polish as you grow.

The Top 10 Fastest to Monetize in 30 Days

If you're impatient for your first sale, these ideas can go from concept to cash quickly. They require minimal setup, low upfront cost, and skills you can learn in a day or two.

1. **AI Social Media Post Packs** — 30 posts for one niche, delivered in Canva.
2. **Blog Post Writing Service** — Niche-specific posts for SEO and authority.

3. **Product Description Revamps** — Optimized copy for Etsy, Amazon, or Shopify.
4. **Meeting Summary Service** — Zoom call transcriptions + action items.
5. **Localized Ad Campaign Packs** — Geo-targeted ad copy + creative.
6. **Resume & LinkedIn Profile Upgrade** — AI-assisted career polish.
7. **E-book or Guide Creation** — Sell via Gumroad or Amazon KDP.
8. **Custom Midjourney Image Packs** — Icons, covers, or backgrounds.
9. **Keyword & SEO Research Reports** — With content topic suggestions.
10. **Personalized Itinerary Planning** — AI-generated travel plans with maps.

Reality Check:

The secret isn't in picking the "perfect" idea. It's in choosing *something* and testing it in the real world. You'll learn more in 30 days of action than in 300 days of theory.

1. AI Content Creation & Writing

💰 Fast ROI | 🕒 Low Time Investment | 📈 Scalable

AI-assisted writing has evolved into a reliable source of income. Pair tools like **ChatGPT, Claude, and Perplexity** with your expertise for content that's fast, on-target, and monetizable.

1. **Blog & Niche Website Content Packages** 💰 🕒 📈 Create bulk content for niche blogs. Offer 10–20 post bundles, SEO-optimized libraries, or evergreen affiliate articles. Sell on Upwork, Fiverr, or direct.

2. **Ad & Sales Page Copywriting** 💰 📈 Use AI to rapidly draft ad headlines, social ad copy, and bullet points. Test variations for conversion wins.

3. **Email Newsletter Creation & Management** 💰 🕒 📈 Research, write, and format weekly editions for niche or branded newsletters. Add lead magnet creation as an upsell.

4. **AI-Accelerated Ghostwriting** 📈 Produce full-length books, guides, or scripts faster. AI drafts, you refine tone and accuracy.

5. **Social Media Caption & Post Creation** 💰 🕒 Batch-create 30–90 days of posts with AI adaptations for each platform. Specialize by niche

6. **Technical Writing** 📈 AI streamlines formatting and draft creation for manuals and SOPs. You add industry expertise.

7. **Press Release & PR Pitch Writing** 💰 📈 Draft compelling releases and media pitches. Pair with distribution via PRWeb or direct outreach.

8. **SEO Content Writing** 📈 Combine AI keyword research with AI drafting for targeted, rank-ready articles.

9. **Freelance Marketplace Gigs** 💰 🕒 Sell productized services (e.g., "20 Instagram captions in 24 hours") as an "AI Content Strategist."

10. **Long-Form Content Summarization** 💰 🕒 Turn hours of webinars or podcasts into summaries, posts, or recaps.

Pro Tip: The big payouts aren't for "writing" — they're for speed + niche expertise + measurable results.

Category 2 — AI Visual & Design

(💰 High Demand | 🕒 Medium Time | 📈 Scalable)

1. **Custom Brand Identity Packages** — Logos, color palettes, and templates using Midjourney + Canva.
2. **Social Media Graphic Packs** — Subscription-based monthly content kits.
3. **Product Mockups & Packaging Design** — AI renders for e-commerce sellers and campaigns.
4. **Print-on-Demand Art Collections** — Themed digital art for Redbubble, TeeSpring, or Printful.
5. **AI-Generated Stock Photo Libraries** — Niche stock imagery for underrepresented markets.
6. **Digital Wallpaper & Asset Packs** — Bundled desktop/mobile wallpapers and UI elements.
7. **NFT Art Collections (Utility-Driven)** — AI-generated assets for gaming, memberships, or events.

8. **Children's Book Illustration** — Consistent AI-generated characters and scenes.

9. **Custom Resume & Pitch Deck Design** — AI-assisted professional headshots + templates.

10. **Event & Marketing Collateral** — Flyers, banners, and signage for small businesses.

Pro Tip: Tie visuals to measurable business goals — not just "pretty" designs.

Category 3 — AI Audio, Video & Multimedia

(💰 High Profit | 🕒 Medium–High Time | 📈 Explosive Growth)

1. **Short-Form Video Repurposing** — Turn long-form content into TikTok/Reels batches.

2. **Voiceover & Audio Narration** — Audiobooks, explainer videos, and eLearning voice tracks.

3. **AI-Powered Podcast Production** — End-to-end editing, cleanup, and content repurposing.

4. **Video Scriptwriting with AI** — Scripts for YouTube, ads, or social campaigns.

5. **Explainer & Training Video Creation** — AI avatars + narration for corporate or course content.

6. **Subtitle Translation & Localization** — Multi-language captions for videos and webinars.

7. **AI Music & Jingle Creation** — Original jingles and soundtracks for ads, podcasts, or games.

8. **YouTube Automation Channels** — Faceless niche channels monetized via ads and affiliates.

9. **Webinar & Virtual Event Production** — Slide decks, promo clips, captions, and post-event summaries.

10. **Personalized Video Messages** — AI avatars delivering custom promos or greetings.

Pro Tip: Package multimedia work into monthly deliverables for stable recurring revenue.

Category 4 — AI Research & Analysis Services

(💰 B2B Demand | 🕒 Medium Time | 📈 High Retainer Potential)

1. **Market Trend Reports** — Use Perplexity or Claude to compile, summarize, and visualize industry data.

2. **Competitor Analysis Packs** — AI-assisted breakdowns of competitor strengths, weaknesses, and positioning.

3. **SEO & Keyword Research** — Generate long-tail keyword lists with search intent clustering.

4. **Product Review Aggregation** — Pull and summarize customer sentiment from multiple sources.

5. **Survey Data Interpretation** — AI-assisted coding of qualitative responses into actionable insights.

6. **Investment Opportunity Reports** — Compile public data and trends for niche investment ideas.

7. **Academic Paper Summaries** — Summarize and interpret peer-reviewed research for professionals.

8. **Business Case Development** — Use AI to gather stats, case examples, and ROI projections.

9. **Customer Feedback Analysis** — Text-mining reviews, support tickets, and NPS surveys.

10. **Industry Newsletter Curation** — Compile and annotate relevant industry updates for subscribers.

Pro Tip: Package research deliverables as recurring monthly briefs for steady income.

Category 5 — AI Marketing Campaign Services

(💰 Fast ROI | 🕒 Medium Time | 📈 Scalable with Templates)

1. **Ad Creative Testing** — AI to generate 10–20 ad variants for rapid A/B testing.

2. **Funnel Copy & Asset Creation** — AI-assisted emails, landing pages, and thank-you pages.

3. **Social Listening Reports** — AI to track brand mentions and sentiment in real time.

4. **Automated Email Sequences** — Set up nurture campaigns for client products or services.

5. **Seasonal Campaign Packs** — Holiday-themed marketing bundles prepped months in advance.

6. **Brand Voice Development** — Use AI to create tone-of-voice guides for all client channels.

7. **AI-Powered Lead Magnets** — Ebooks, checklists, and mini-courses created at speed.

8. **Content Calendar Creation** — Month-long multi-platform posting schedules.
9. **Affiliate Promotion Assets** — Landing pages, emails, and banners for affiliate launches.
10. **Localized Campaign Translations** — AI translation + cultural adaptation for global reach.

Pro Tip: Fast turnaround is your edge — businesses pay for speed in marketing.

Category 6 — AI Admin & Productivity Services

(💰 Steady Demand | 🕒 Low Time | 📈 Retainer-Friendly)

1. **Inbox Management & Email Drafting** — AI-assisted sorting and reply drafting.
2. **Meeting Summaries & Action Logs** — Real-time transcription and task extraction.
3. **Document Formatting & Cleanup** — Standardizing templates and layouts.
4. **CRM Data Entry & Enrichment** — Updating contact records with AI lookups.
5. **Calendar Management** — Auto-scheduling and smart meeting prep.
6. **Expense Categorization** — AI to process and sort receipts or bank transactions.
7. **Proposal & Contract Drafting** — AI-assisted boilerplate creation with client customization.

8. **Hiring & Applicant Screening** — Resume analysis and shortlist creation.

9. **Internal Process Documentation** — SOP writing from interviews or recordings.

10. **Personal Knowledge Base Building** — Organizing notes and research for busy executives.

Pro Tip: Offer "virtual AI assistant" packages — not just task-by-task billing.

Category 7 — AI Data Cleanup & Automation

(Niche Skill | Medium Time | High Repeat Value)

1. **Spreadsheet Cleanup** — Standardizing formats, fixing formulas, and removing duplicates.

2. **Data Extraction from PDFs** — Pull structured data from unstructured sources.

3. **Web Scraping & Formatting** — Automated pulling of public info into usable CSV files.

4. **CRM Data Migration** — Cleaning and mapping data for system switches.

5. **API-Based Report Generation** — Auto-pulling reports from multiple sources.

6. **KPI Dashboard Setup** — Connect Google Sheets, Looker, or Power BI to AI data flows.

7. **Email List Hygiene** — De-duplication and bounce removal.

8. **AI-Driven Data Categorization** — Tagging content or products for easier search.

9. **Survey Data Cleaning** — Prepping raw survey exports for analysis.

10. **Image Metadata Tagging** — AI labeling for large photo libraries.

Pro Tip: Data cleanup is invisible work — clients often pay a premium for "pain removal."

Category 8 — AI-Powered E-commerce Services

(💰 High ROI | 🕒 Medium Time | 📈 Product-Based Scaling)

1. **Product Description Optimization** — SEO-rich, AI-polished product copy.

2. **Upsell & Cross-Sell Email Flows** — Automated follow-up sequences for buyers.

3. **Product Photo Background Editing** — AI cleanup or replacement for listing consistency.

4. **Review Reply Automation** — On-brand, human-like responses to customer feedback.

5. **Competitor Price Tracking** — AI monitoring with alert triggers.

6. **Bulk Product Upload Prep** — Cleaning and formatting CSVs for marketplaces.

7. **PPC Ad Asset Generation** — Headlines, copy, and creative concepts.

8. **Chatbot Product Recommendations** — AI sales assistants for Shopify or WooCommerce.

9. **Customer Service Macros** — AI drafting canned but personalized replies.

10. **Seasonal Product Trend Reports** — Identifying products to push based on data.

Pro Tip: Pair AI services with revenue-linked pricing for bigger upside.

Category 9 — AI Education & Training

(💰 Growing Market | 🕒 Medium Time | 📈 Evergreen Demand)

1. **AI Skills Workshops** — Teach ChatGPT, Midjourney, or AI automation basics.

2. **Corporate AI Training** — In-house sessions on integrating AI tools.

3. **Paid Webinars** — Topic-specific live or recorded events.

4. **AI Course Creation** — Evergreen video courses on Udemy or Gumroad.

5. **Membership Communities** — Paid groups with weekly AI tips.

6. **Local Meetups & Bootcamps** — Charge for live, in-person AI training.

7. **One-on-One Coaching** — Tailored sessions for creators or business owners.

8. **AI Prompt Libraries** — Sell curated, niche-specific prompt packs.

9. **Certification Programs** — Offer niche AI skill badges.

10. **AI for Kids Classes** — Parent-funded STEM learning.

Pro Tip: Pair education with templates or tools so it's not "knowledge-only."

Category 10 — AI SaaS & Digital Tools

(💰 High Scalability | 🕒 Long-Term Build | 📈 Recurring Revenue)

1. **Niche SaaS Apps** — Solve specific problems with a lightweight AI app.

2. **White-Label AI Tools** — Brand existing tools for niche markets.

3. **Template Marketplaces** — Sell AI-generated templates for Notion, Canva, or Figma.

4. **API Microservices** — Build small tools that plug into larger platforms.

5. **Automated PDF Report Generators** — Subscription-based industry reports.

6. **Custom Chatbots** — Niche conversational bots for businesses.

7. **AI Integration Plugins** — Extensions for WordPress, Shopify, or CRMs.

8. **Niche AI Data Feeds** — Sell curated datasets.

9. **Scriptable Automation Tools** — Command-line tools for developers.

10. **AI-Powered Calculators** — ROI calculators, cost estimators, or personalized planners.

Pro Tip: Even a micro-tool with 200 paying users at $15/mo = $36,000/year.

Category 11 — AI-Enhanced Freelance Services

(💰 Flexible | 🕒 Low–Medium Time | 📈 Client Base Growth)

1. **Proposal Writing** — Faster, sharper client proposals with AI drafting.

2. **Project Plan Creation** — Gantt charts and milestone mapping.

3. **Grant Writing** — AI-assisted research and drafting for funding applications.

4. **Resume Optimization** — AI keyword matching for ATS systems.

5. **LinkedIn Profile Revamps** — Position clients for more inbound leads.

6. **Speechwriting** — AI-assisted political or corporate speech drafts.

7. **Event Planning Docs** — AI-generated run sheets, checklists, and timelines.

8. **Press Kit Assembly** — Combine bios, product shots, and media blurbs.

9. **Creative Brainstorm Facilitation** — AI-generated concept lists for campaigns.

10. **Technical Proposals** — AI-assisted requirements documents for projects.

Category 12 — AI Personalization Services

(💰 High Engagement | 🕒 Medium Time | 📈 Repeat Buyers)

1. **Personalized Gift Recommendations** — AI-generated based on recipient data.

2. **Custom Meal Planning** — Dietary AI plans with grocery lists.

3. **Fitness Plan Creation** — Personalized exercise programming.

4. **Style & Wardrobe Curation** — AI suggestions paired with affiliate links.

5. **AI Travel Itinerary Planning** — Multi-day, interest-based itineraries.

6. **Pet Care Plans** — Breed- and health-specific guidance.

7. **Learning Path Recommendations** — Skill-building roadmaps.

8. **Reading List Curation** — Tailored book lists with summaries.

9. **Home Organization Plans** — AI-generated step-by-step declutter schedules.

10. **Parenting Tip Collections** — Stage-specific activity and guidance packs.

Category 13 — AI for Real Estate

(High Ticket | Medium Time | Commission-Boosting)

1. **Listing Description Optimization** — High-converting property writeups.
2. **Neighborhood Data Reports** — AI-assisted school, safety, and lifestyle summaries.
3. **Virtual Staging Images** — AI-generated decor swaps for listing photos.
4. **Client Nurture Email Sequences** — Pre-written, seasonal, and local tips.
5. **Real Estate Market Reports** — Local trend analysis and predictions.
6. **Property Comparison Sheets** — AI-generated feature comparison tables.
7. **Social Media Post Creation** — Branded, geo-targeted content batches.
8. **Lead Magnet Creation** — Free reports to attract and capture leads.
9. **Post-Sale Follow-Up Kits** — Automated follow-up systems for referrals.
10. **Open House Promo Packages** — Flyers, social ads, and signage.

Category 14 — AI Licensing & Asset Sales

(💰 Passive Income | 🕒 Build Once | 📈 Long-Term Sales)

1. **Stock Asset Creation** — AI-generated images, icons, or music.
2. **Licensable Prompt Libraries** — Sell to other creators or agencies.
3. **Template Licensing** — Resell templates with commercial rights.
4. **White-Label Course Content** — Sell educational materials under license.
5. **Dataset Licensing** — Curated niche datasets for model training.
6. **Tool Reskinning & Resale** — Customize and resell open-source AI tools.
7. **Custom Illustration Packs** — Bundle thematic sets for resale.
8. **Digital Pattern Libraries** — Textures for 3D artists, designers, and printers.
9. **Exclusive Design Commissions** — Sell one-time rights at premium pricing.
10. **Music & Sound Effect Libraries** — AI-generated and royalty-free.

Recommended Tools & Resources

These are battle-tested AI tools, platforms, and learning hubs you can use right now to start, grow, and scale your AI-powered income streams. They're grouped by what you'll be doing — not by company hype.

All-in-One AI Platforms

These are your Swiss Army knives — text, image, code, and more in one place.

- **ChatGPT (OpenAI)** – Best general-purpose AI for writing, research, and workflows.
- **Claude (Anthropic)** – Long-context reasoning, great for analyzing large documents.
- **Gemini (Google DeepMind)** – Fast search-integrated AI, great for fact-checking.
- **Perplexity** – AI + live web search with source links (ideal for up-to-date research).

Prompting & Workflow Tools

For structuring, organizing, and scaling your AI prompts.

- **AIPRM** – Curated prompt library for ChatGPT.

- **FlowGPT** – Searchable community of tested prompts.
- **PromptPerfect** – Optimizes prompts for better results across AI models.
- **Make** – No-code automation platform to chain AI tools together.
- **Zapier** – Connects AI tools to your apps and workflows.

Content Creation Tools

Blog posts, ad copy, scripts, and more — at scale.

- **Jasper** – AI writing with built-in templates for marketing.
- **Writesonic** – Quick content generation with SEO features.
- **Copy.ai** – Simple, fast ad and sales copy creation.
- **Surfer SEO** – Optimizes AI content for search rankings.

Image & Design Tools

From AI art to product mockups and branded visuals.

- **Midjourney** – Best for high-quality, stylized AI art.
- **DALL·E 3** – Inside ChatGPT, great for conceptual and illustrative art.
- **Leonardo.ai** – Commercial-friendly AI image generation.
- **Canva** – Graphic design + AI features for social and marketing assets.
- **Kittl** – AI-assisted typography and merch-ready designs.

Video & Audio Tools

For YouTube channels, marketing videos, and social clips.

- **Runway** – Text-to-video, video editing, and effects.
- **Pika** – Fast AI video generation from prompts.
- **Descript** – Edit videos like text; AI-powered transcription & overdub.
- **OpusClip** – Turns long videos into social-ready clips.
- **ElevenLabs** – Best AI voice cloning and narration.

Data, Research & Analysis Tools

For fact-checking, number crunching, and insights.

- **Perplexity** – Live data + citation-based search.
- **DataGPT** – Natural language data analysis.
- **Excel + ChatGPT Plugins** – AI-powered spreadsheet automation.
- **Notion AI** – Research summarization + personal knowledge base.

Business & E-Commerce Tools

For selling services, products, or digital downloads.

- **Gumroad** – Sell digital products directly.
- **Etsy** – Marketplace for printables, templates, and digital art.

- **Shopify** – E-commerce platform with AI tools.
- **Fiverr / Upwork** – Freelance marketplaces for AI services.
- **ThriveCart** – Checkout and course hosting platform.

Learning & Skill-Building

Stay ahead by continuously leveling up.

- **TheresAnAIForThat.com** – Database of AI tools by category.
- **LearnPrompting.org** – Free prompt engineering lessons.
- **Futurepedia.io** – Updated AI tool directory.
- **YouTube Channels** – Matt Wolfe, The Futur, Two Minute Papers (AI news & tutorials).

Don't just "use tools" — build a system. Pick one primary AI platform, two specialized tools, and one automation connector. Learn them deeply, and you'll outperform 90% of people chasing the next shiny app.

Thank You

You could have picked from hundreds of other books, but you bought mine, and I appreciate it. Thank you so much for purchasing my book.

If you enjoyed my book (I hope you did!), can I ask you for a tiny favor? Can you please post a review on the platform? Posting a review is the best way to support the work of independent authors like me.

Your feedback will help me continue writing books that will help you achieve your desired results. It means a lot to me to hear from you.

I am happy for anyone to reach out to me for help, comments, collaboration ideas, or feedback at

brian@brianscottfitzgerald.com

Visit my author page with this link or Scan this QR code

https://www.amazon.com/author/brianscottfitzgerald.

www.ingramcontent.com/pod-product-compliance
Lightning Source LLC
LaVergne TN
LVHW100307210926
848480LV00003B/1048